INVISIBLE WAR WOUNDS

Joe Wilson Barrett Jungeblodt

This book is for informational purposes only. It is not intended to serve as a substitute for professional medical advice.

The author and publisher specifically disclaim any, and all liability, arising, directly or indirectly from the use of any information contained in this book.

A Healthcare professional should be consulted regarding your specific medical situation.

Invisible War Wounds copyright © 2024 by Joe
ISBN: 9798342096492
Independently published

All rights reserved. No part of this book may be used or reproduced in any manner whatsoever without written permission of the publisher.

The views and opinions expressed are those of the author alone and should not be taken to represent those of His Majesty's Government, MOD, HM Armed Forces or any government agency.

The last chapter of my book provides a brief overview of the medical conditions and terms I've encountered, designed to save you the hassle of searching online or asking Alexa for answers.

Thank you, Sammy, for editing and "getting my book out there".

Thanks babe, love ya.

Tom & Sam, love you guys.

Trigger Warning

Before you begin reading this book, it's important to be aware that it contains content that may be distressing or triggering for some readers. Some of the topics covered include:

- Different Accounts of My Time in War Zones: The book recounts various experiences from time spent in war zones.
- Suicide: The book discusses thoughts and experiences related to suicide.
- Depression: The book explores first-hand experiences with severe depression.
- Anxiety: Accounts of anxiety, including its impact on daily life are discussed.
- PTSD (Post-Traumatic Stress Disorder): The book delves into the struggles and symptoms associated with PTSD.
- Heart Attack: Experiences related to heart attacks are mentioned in detail.
- Panic Attack: The book describes episodes of panic attacks and their effects.
- Numerous Different Medical Procedures: The book discusses various medical procedures that may be detailed or intense.

These topics are handled with care and sensitivity, but they may still evoke strong emotions or memories. Please take care of your well-being as you read and consider whether this content is right for you. If you find any part of the book distressing, I encourage you to seek support from a trusted friend, family member, or mental health professional.

What is Mental Health?

Mental Health affects how we think, feel, and act. It also helps determine how we handle stress, relate to others, and make healthy choices. Mental health is important at every stage of life, from childhood and adolescence through adulthood.

Mental illness

Typically, has more of a significant detrimental impact across many areas of an individual's life than episodes of poor mental health which may be situation specific or time limited.

Anyone of any age, gender, geographical background, race, ethnicity, class, background, religion, education, economic status, spirituality, sexual orientation can experience a mental illness.

Foreword - 1

"Invisible War Wounds"

"Invisible War Wounds" is written by my oldest friend and provides a glimpse into not only the challenges of serving your Country for 24 years, but also the period after you leave. The toll that service has had on your physical body and of course your mind.

I first met Joe in 1987 whilst we were both serving in Münster West Germany. We attended several courses together and although I had been posted away, by some twist of fate we both ended up in the same Battery of the same Regiment in late 1993. We were firm friends in the past but became best mates thereafter and as the saying goes "the rest is history."

Although we were inseparable for many years, my career went off in another direction and was posted to the UK for the last two years of my service. Despite the distance between us we stayed close and that is still true to this very day.

In this book Joe shares some good and bad memories of his service, but if he were to document everything we got up to, that would be another entirely different book. Most of us just remember the good times and tend to blank out the tough times, but some Squaddies are unable to use this filter.

Joe has always been filled with self-confidence and a single mindedness that is obviously apparent when you look at his Army career.

The biggest shock for me was that my best friend, with all the positive mental strength that I had witnessed over many years, would be struck down by depression and anxiety. Which ultimately led him to take the unprecedented decision to admit himself to a mental health hospital for treatment.

Joe's story offers a stark reminder of how fragile the human mind can be and that the strongest of us could be affected at some time in our lives.

Joe is now coming out the other side and I take my hat off to my old friend for his courage and resilience during what can only be described as the toughest fight of his life.

Warrant Officer Paul (Harry) Harrison

Foreword - 2

"Invisible War Wounds"

"Invisible War Wounds" provides a touching glimpse into the challenging yet transformative journey of a British soldier.

Through the lens of his personal story, readers are invited to explore the complex landscape of army life—a world filled with both hardships and triumphs, challenges and successes.

From the relentless physical and mental rigours of constant training for war to the harrowing reality of operational deployments and the strain it places on family dynamics, the writers story encapsulates the multifaceted nature of military existence.

As the story unfolds, the reader bears witness to the profound toll exacted by the relentless demands of military service.

The writer grapples not only with the physical challenges of combat readiness but also with the unseen scars left by the psychological trauma of war.

Yet, amidst the trials and tribulations, moments of resilience and camaraderie appear, offering glimpses of light amidst the darkness. The story takes an unexpected turn as the writer confronts a new adversary—the silent assailant of a heart attack and mental health struggles.

From the heights of being the" Karaoke King" to a "mental health hospital", battling depression, anxiety and PTSD the writers journey serves as a stark reminder of the fragility of human resilience and the importance of seeking support in times of need.

Through "Invisible War Wounds", readers are given a poignant insight into the realities of life—both within the structured confines of military service and beyond.

It is a story that transcends borders and boundaries, offering a universal message of courage, resilience, and the enduring power of the human spirit to overcome even the most formidable of challenges.

In its raw authenticity, this story serves as a testament to the stalwart nature of the human experience—a journey marked by triumphs, setbacks, and the relentless pursuit of hope and healing.

"A friend"

Contents

PART VII: My advice

Introduction

Navigating the treacherous terrain of mental illness has been, and continues to be, an arduous journey that has affected every phase of my life. From the innocent days of childhood to the battle-hardened years of my 24-year military career and eventual transition to civilian life.

Each step of my thrilling (yet sometimes bizarre) path has been marked by its own trials and tribulations, leading me to confront demons both seen and unseen. Yet, amidst the shadows cast by the spectres of severe depression, anxiety and PTSD there is still a resilience born of survival—a resilience that persists as I navigate the challenges of the present day.

From the crucible of my heart attack to the ongoing struggle with the invisible scars of war, my story is one of endurance, of grappling with darkness in pursuit of the flickering light of hope.

As I reflect on my journey, I feel compelled to share it with you, hoping to convey a message of solidarity and empathy. Life has taken me through twists and turns, highs and lows, moments of triumph and moments of despair. Yet, through it all, one constant stays: the understanding that we are never truly alone in our struggles. So, I extend my hand to you, inviting you to join me in embracing the shared human experience, finding strength in our collective resilience, and realising that amidst the chaos

You are not alone.

In the height of my accomplishments, I felt an invincibility coursing through my veins. I had conquered obstacles, achieved milestones. Yet, the insidious grip of mental illness blindsided me, shattering my illusions of invulnerability. In my ignorance, I had underestimated the power and complexity of the human mind, unaware of the invisible war wounds it could inflict.

The onset of severe depression, anxiety and PTSD left me reeling, struggling to understand the turmoil raging within me.

Even now, as I grapple with these demons, I am humbled by the vast depths of the mind's ability for both agony and resilience. Though the journey is still fraught with uncertainties, I cling to the knowledge that understanding is the first step towards healing and reclaiming control of my life.

Preface

Mental health is undeniably a central theme of my book, but it is not its sole focus. The first chapters serve as an introduction to the real me, offering a glimpse into my life before the unexpected and often inexplicable downturn that would later unfold.

The pages that follow are not the product of detached observation or academic study; they are the raw and unfiltered chronicles of my own harrowing journey with severe depression, anxiety and PTSD. Tackling these demons has been, and still is—though not as intensely—an agonising and deeply personal struggle, one that defies easy explanation or understanding.

I've grown weary of the well-meaning yet inadequate phrase, "I can only imagine," for no amount of imagination can truly capture the pain and confusion that accompanies mental illness. While my mental health professionals have undoubtedly had my best interests at heart, their empathy and support can only go so far, as they have not traversed the treacherous terrain of despair and anguish that I have come to know intimately.

In writing this book, my aim is not to elicit pity or sympathy, but rather to offer a frank and illuminating account of an experience that profoundly altered the course of my life. Until it blindsided me, I was unaware of the intricate complexities and challenges that come with mental health struggles.

In a world that often feels overwhelmingly bleak and hopeless, my journey has been marked by moments of profound darkness and despair, yet also by glimmers of resilience and hope that have sustained me through the darkest of times. I only wish there had been something like my book available when I was fighting my demons.

My hope is that by sharing my story, I can offer some comfort and understanding to those who are navigating their own mental health struggles and provide the guidance and companionship I so desperately needed. Through these pages, I seek to share my journey in relatable, layman's terms, tracing the origins of my mental illnesses and charting the arduous path toward healing and understanding.

It's important to acknowledge that this book serves solely as a source of information and should not be regarded as a substitute for professional medical advice.

While I draw upon my personal experiences to provide insight and guidance, it's essential for individuals facing mental health challenges to seek support from qualified professionals.

Every individual's journey is unique, and professional guidance can offer tailored solutions and comprehensive support to navigate through difficult times.

Why?

When people ask me why I chose to combine a mental health book with my autobiography, I often reflect on my own journey—one marked by both the triumphs and the unexpected, often harsh, realities of life. As someone who has worn many hats—soldier, husband, father and self-proclaimed "tough guy"—I never imagined I would face the challenges that came with mental illness. Yet, like so many others, I found myself blindsided.

A Shocking Reality: Mental Illness Can Affect Anyone

For a long time, I believed that mental illness was something that happened to other people, not to someone like me who had seen combat, led others, and faced down physical dangers. I thought my experiences in the military, with its emphasis on toughness and resilience, had hardened me against anything life could throw my way. But mental illness doesn't discriminate based on your perceived strength or the life experiences that should have made you immune.

The day I realised something was deeply wrong was a turning point, a moment that shattered my preconceived notions about mental health. The truth is, it can happen to anyone—even those of us who believe we are the least likely to be affected. I was forced to confront a reality that I had never prepared for, and it was terrifying. This is why I felt it was crucial to write about my experience and to combine my story with practical insights into mental health.

The Intersection of Experience and Education

Writing an autobiography is an intimate act, one that exposes your life to the world. But combining it with a mental health book was about more than just sharing my story; it was about using my experience to educate and, hopefully, to help others who might be walking a similar path.

Mental health can often feel like an abstract concept until it touches you personally. By blending my life's story with information and guidance on mental health, I wanted to create something that could resonate on multiple levels. The personal stories in my autobiography serve as case studies, showing how mental illness can manifest in the life of someone who, by all accounts, should have been able to handle anything.

It's one thing to read about the symptoms of depression, anxiety, or PTSD in a textbook, but it's another to see how those symptoms played out in my life. By doing this, I hope to bridge the gap between clinical understanding and personal experience, making mental health issues more relatable and less stigmatised.

Breaking Down the Stigma

Stigma remains one of the biggest barriers to mental health awareness and treatment. As a former soldier, I know all too well the culture of silence and toughness that pervades environments like the military. Admitting to struggling with mental health issues can be seen as a sign of weakness, something to be ashamed of.

In combining my story with a mental health book, I wanted to challenge this stigma head-on. My message is clear: if someone like me—a person who prided himself on being strong, resilient, and unshakable—can face mental health challenges, then it's okay for others to acknowledge their struggles too. There is no shame in admitting that you need help, and there is strength in seeking it out.

By sharing my journey, I hope to encourage others, especially those who might see themselves in my story, to take their mental health seriously and to understand that it's not a battle they have to fight alone.

A Journey of Self-Discovery and Healing

Writing this book was as much a process of self-discovery and healing for me as it was a tool for helping others. It forced me to confront my past, to unpack the experiences that led me to where I am today, and to better understand how my mental health was shaped by those experiences.

In doing so, I've learned a great deal about myself—lessons that I might never have uncovered if I hadn't decided to write this book. The process has been cathartic, allowing me to make peace with parts of my life that I had buried deep down.

For readers, I hope this dual narrative provides not just insight, but also comfort. Mental illness can make you feel isolated, but by sharing my story, I want to show that you are not alone. There are others who have walked this path and come out on the other side, and there is hope for healing and recovery.

My decision to combine a mental health book with my autobiography was driven by a desire to make a difference. I wanted to provide a resource that was grounded in real-life experience, one that could serve as both a guide and a source of inspiration.

If my story can help even one person feel less alone, if it can encourage someone to seek help or to start a conversation about mental health, then I will have achieved what I set out to do.

Mental illness is not a sign of weakness; it's a reality of life that many of us will face at some point. By sharing my journey, I hope to contribute to a broader understanding and to help break down the walls of stigma and silence that still surround mental health today.

Even if you aren't dealing with mental health problems yourself, I believe in the saying, "To be forewarned is to be forearmed." Knowing about these issues can help you be better prepared if they ever affect you or someone you care about. I also believe that "

"Knowledge is power."

Invisible War Wounds

In life's tough trials, things may shatter,
From bones to hearts, under pressure's chatter.
Invisible War Wounds, etched deep within,
Scarring our souls, where do we begin?

Mental illness, a silent strife,
Hidden from view yet carving our life.
Like a fractured bone, healing's slow pace,
But mental health battles, an endless race.

Wounds may linger, unseen and unheard,
Yet they weigh heavy, like a whispered word.
The journey's tough, far from serene,
But in the darkness, a light may gleam.

Each day a fight, a battle to brave,
Learning to cope, to ride each wave.
Though the road is long, and healing's slow,
Strength within, it begins to grow.

For in our brokenness, we find our might,
Invisible War Wounds, they shape our sight.
Though scars may linger, we learn to rise,
In the face of adversity, we claim our prize.

So let us stand tall, amidst thc pain,
Invisible War Wounds, they leave their stain.
With each passing day, we learn and grow,
In the depths of darkness, we continue to glow.

PART I:
The Beginning

Chapter 1

My Early Years

Born in the vibrant city of Liverpool in 1968, I found myself nestled between an elder brother and a younger sister, occupying the role of the quintessential middle child. While the specifics of my early years elude my memory, I am keenly aware that they were marked by adversity and challenges.

Growing up in a household where resources were scarce, I learned the value of resilience and determination from an early age.

Though the details may be hazy, the echoes of those formative years continue to shape my perspective on life, imbuing me with a sense of perseverance and tenacity that has guided me through both trials and triumphs.

No mobile phones, no internet, my school uniform was my brother's, "hand-me-downs" and not much money to go round. I do remember living in a council house that backed on to a massive playing field. There was a slide, a roundabout and a seesaw. I spent most of my free time in this massive open space and I remember my mum shouting, "tea's ready" from our back garden.

Growing up, my father's presence was often brief due to his demanding shifts at Moss Side Hospital, conveniently located just a brisk 10-minute walk from our home.

Despite the limited time we spent together, one cherished memory stands out vividly in my mind.

After his night shifts, I eagerly awaited his return, expecting the simple yet heartfelt gesture he never failed to deliver: a penguin fruit and nut chocolate bar saved from his packed lunch.

In the backdrop of my early years, the scene around the coal fire painted a picture of resilience and solidarity. The three of us seeking warmth and sharing a humble bowl of "Ready Brek" with warm milk and water, while holding our school shirts close to the flames, oblivious to any other way of life.

These were times marked by hardship, where the word "love" remained a foreign concept, unfamiliar to our vocabulary.

One of my most cherished childhood memories revolves around our annual two-week holiday in Looe, Cornwall. The adventure began under the cloak of night, with our family car, a VW Beetle, packed to the brim and a trailer hitched to the back, embarking on the journey to our temporary home—a caravan.

Despite the anticipation that filled the air, me and my brother inevitably found ourselves entangled in backseat battles, our squabbles casting a shadow of exasperation over our parents. These petty fights, a ritual of sorts, seemed to spoil the holiday before it even started.

As I sift through the fragments of my childhood memories, I find them shrouded in ambiguity, as if painted with broad strokes of selective recollection.

Amidst the haze, certain emotions appear vividly, chief among them the persistent sense of loneliness and the struggles I faced with academic subjects.

While my mind seems to have blurred the details, there were bright spots: moments of triumph on the canvas and field, where my talents in art and sport shone through.

The relentless battles between me and my brother remain etched in my memory, each clash escalating in intensity until it reached a tipping point that even alarmed my own mother.

I recall the day she reached her breaking point, dialling 999 in a panicked attempt to prevent what she feared could result in serious harm. In a blur of flashing lights and blaring sirens, a police car tore down our street, arriving to quell the turmoil that had erupted within our home.

Standing before us, a stern-faced officer delivered a scolding that left us guilt ridden, a stark reminder of the consequences of our constant squabbles and the need to temper our combative spirits before it spiralled out of control.

The concept of pocket money in my upbringing often felt elusive, either conveniently "forgotten" or scarcely enough to indulge in a simple treat from the local shop.

Left to navigate the world with little financial support, I learned the value of self-reliance early on. From juggling weekend work to before and after school jobs—ranging from a paper round to guarding a chicken delivery lorry in Toxteth. *

I embraced every opportunity to earn a few extra quid. Yet, amidst the hustle, there lingered a sense of resentment as I watched a part of my hard-earned cash slip away, surrendered to my mother's coffers as a contribution to my, "food and board," a reminder of the sacrifices made in the pursuit of financial stability.

*The Toxteth riots of July 1981 cast a shadow over the inner-city streets of Liverpool. Particularly in the neighbourhood of Toxteth, leaving an indelible mark on both the community and the collective consciousness of the nation. Born from the simmering tensions between the local police force and the marginalised black community, the riots were a manifestation of years of systemic neglect, discrimination and social inequality. Sparked by a singular incident but fuelled by deep-rooted grievances, the uprising laid bare the fractures within society and the urgent need for meaningful dialogue and change. In the aftermath of the turmoil, scars remained etched upon the landscape, serving as a stark reminder of the unresolved issues that continued to plague urban communities across the country.

Chapter 2

Accepting God into my life

Growing up in a household where religion held a firm grip, I grappled with the weight of expectations imposed upon me. The constant pressure to adhere to strict beliefs and practices felt suffocating, casting a shadow over my formative years. Yet, amidst the constraints, there were moments of solace and connection found within the walls of the church.

Sunday school provided a sanctuary where I could explore faith on my own terms, while Friday nights became an opportunity to forge friendships and engage in wholesome activities like table tennis and football.

It was during a twelve-day summer camp, surrounded in the warmth of fellowship, this drew me to the cradle of Christianity. Accepting Jesus Christ into my life inspired me with a sense of purpose and belonging, filling a void that I couldn't quite explain. Though the reasons remained elusive, the newfound faith brought a profound sense of peace and fulfilment, anchoring me in a troubled world and offering a beacon of hope in the darkest of times. However, as time passed, my journey diverged from the confines of the church.

In the pages ahead, I will delve into the reasons behind my gradual severance, and ultimate rejection of the belief in a higher power.

Chapter 3

Something missing

At the tender age of fourteen, I was still grappling with a sense of emptiness, unsure of how to fill the void in my life. It was then that I stumbled upon a path that would ultimately shape my future – I joined the army cadets.

From the moment I stepped foot into the cadet hall, I knew I had found my calling. The camaraderie, discipline and sense of purpose resonated deeply with me, igniting a passion that would only grow stronger with time.

Meeting once a week, we delved into many different activities, each designed to cultivate skills essential for military life. From mastering drill formations, hands-on experience with the Lee-Enfield 303 rifle during skill at arms training to honing our map reading abilities, every session offered a new challenge and opportunity for growth.

The monthly excursions to Skelmersdale Transit army camp provided an immersive experience unlike any other. Spending nights under the stars, devouring army rations, and engaging in unbridled camaraderie allowed me to immerse myself fully in the military lifestyle. It was here, amidst the tranquil embrace of the forest, that I felt most at home – free to express myself. In these moments, I discovered a sense of belonging and purpose that had long eluded me, solidifying my commitment to a life of service.

Many Tales to Tell

With 24 years of service in the army, I've accumulated a mountain worth of poignant and memorable stories that encapsulate the breadth of my experiences.

While I have many tales to tell, the daunting task of completing a book looms large, and I'm uncertain if it will ever come to fruition.

I am privileged to share a selection of my stories with you. Each story I recount from my years of service holds a profound significance, etched vividly in my memory.

These experiences have shaped my perspective, instilled lessons of resilience and courage, and deepened my appreciation for the bonds forged in the crucible of military life. From moments of triumph to trials of adversity, each narrative carries its weight of emotion, leaving an indelible mark on my journey. Through sharing these stories, I hope to convey not just the events themselves, but also the profound impact they have had on shaping who I am today.

I am profoundly grateful for the opportunity to share them with you.

The bit, no one talks about

Life as a soldier deployed on an operational tour, is undeniably a gruelling journey but amidst the hardships, there's also a profound sense of accomplishment and purpose.

Every challenge faced brings with it a unique opportunity to make a difference and save lives, which adds a significant layer of meaning to the experience.

Having personally experienced these hardships on multiple occasions; I am living proof to the immense sense of achievement that comes from overcoming obstacles and persevering in the face of adversity.

Whether it's enduring extreme weather conditions, navigating volatile situations, or being separated from the comforts of home, every trial faced serves as proof to the resilience and strength of the human spirit.

The sense of fulfilment that comes from knowing that your actions have made a positive impact cannot be overstated. Whether it's providing aid to those in need, protecting innocent civilians, or contributing to the larger mission of peace and stability, each soldier plays a vital role in shaping the outcome of their deployment.

Every day brings forth a fresh set of obstacles, from navigating through harsh climates to grappling with the absence of basic amenities.

I've witnessed first-hand the devastating impact of illnesses like Diarrhoea and Vomiting (D&V), which have the potential to incapacitate entire regiments, emphasising the critical importance of maintaining personal hygiene in such harsh environments. Even minor lapses in hygiene can lead to severe consequences, as exemplified by an incident in Kuwait where a soldier suffered serious burns from falling asleep under the scorching sun and was hospitalised, underscoring the need for vigilance and self-care.

Soldiers confront an unforgiving adversary in the form of weather, which has the power to transform ordinary tasks into formidable challenges.

The desert is a harsh and unforgiving terrain where the landscape stretches endlessly, dominated by vast expanses of sand and rock. Not a cloud in sight the sun's rays beating down without mercy. The air hangs heavy and suffocating, enveloping you like a dense blanket, making even the simplest movements feel laborious.

In every direction, the landscape is a sea of sand and sky, stretching infinitely towards the horizon, creating feelings of loneliness and emptiness. The intense heat causes the ground to shimmer and crackle in the distance.

When temperatures soar, the way we see things can get a bit wonky due to heat haze and mirages. These optical illusions create shimmering waves or ripples in the air, especially noticeable above hot surfaces like roads or sandy areas.

In addition to the boiling temperatures, soldiers must contend with the relentless onslaught of mosquitoes, whose buzzing and biting can leave painful welts all over your body. To combat these pests, we rely on mosquito repellents like "Off," but even these measures come with their own discomforts.

The sting of the repellent on the skin can feel like jumping into a pool of electrolytes, highlighting the extreme measures required to endure and survive in such environments.

On the other end of the spectrum, freezing temperatures bring the threat of frostbite, turning even the simplest tasks into struggles for survival. Despite lacking means to stay warm, soldiers must adapt to their circumstances, often relying on the warmth generated by simply moving or running on the spot.

The unpredictable nature of weather further compounds the demands of a soldier's job, with driving rain adding to the difficulties, particularly when shelter or means of drying clothing are scarce.

Preparation is key for soldiers, as you must be ready to face whatever nature throws our way. Failing to anticipate the weather's wrath can have dire consequences, highlighting the necessity of packing the right gear.

Additionally, soldiers often find themselves deployed in war-torn countries where modern comforts are but a distant memory. Obtaining necessities becomes a Herculean task, with access to shops non-existent. Living without essentials like running water, electricity and proper sanitation further worsens the challenges soldiers face, forcing them to rely on BBC World News for information about the outside world.

Fatigue poses a significant threat, whether due to the intentional stresses of war or the inability to sleep amidst adverse conditions. The strain of exhaustion can impair decision-making and diminish performance, affecting not only oneself but others around you.

In addition to the challenges mentioned above, we also contend with another significant "inconvenience", an overpowering smell.

Whether it's the stench of human waste being disposed of in rivers or the foul odour of unmanaged waste piles in towns, the pervasive smell adds an extra layer of discomfort.

Despite these challenges, soldiers carry the weight of their mission with unwavering determination. Whether tasked with maintaining peace or removing a dictator during tumultuous times, soldiers navigate through volatile situations with a deep sense of purpose and resolve. Their ability to thrive amidst adversity earns them the title of a unique breed of "animal" reflecting their unparalleled strength and resilience in the face of hardship.

Chapter 4

Boy Soldier: 1984

The army cadets served as the cornerstone for my journey toward a career as a regular soldier.

The journey into military service often begins with a pivotal moment of decision, one that can shape the trajectory of one's life in unforeseen ways. For me, that moment came with the requirement of written permission (as I was only a boy - 15 years old) from my parents to join JLRRA (Junior Leaders Regiment Royal Artillery).

Reflecting, I still find myself grappling with the uncertainty surrounding their motivation for signing the consent form.

Even to this day, the exact reason is still elusive, shrouded in the mystery of parental discretion and the innate complexities of familial dynamics. Yet, amidst the ambiguity, I embarked on a path that would irrevocably alter my course, marked by the trials and triumphs inherent in the journey of military service.

At the age of sixteen, I eagerly joined the Junior Leaders Regiment Royal Artillery at Bramcote in Birmingham, embarking on a transformative chapter of my life.

Reflecting on my time spent at Bramcote, I am struck by the stark contrast between the exhilarating experiences and the rigorous structure reminiscent of a Military Corrective Training Facility. * (MCTC)

*MCTC - The principal function of the MCTC is to detain personnel, (Imprisonment) both male and female, from the three Services and civilians subject to the Armed Forces Act.

For twelve months, I was immersed in a dynamic environment, sharing quarters with thirty fellow recruits, each with their own unique background and story to tell.

The atmosphere was full of energy, as alpha personalities cycled through our ranks regularly, each competing for dominance within our tightly knit community.

Despite the challenges, I embraced the opportunity for growth and advancement, earning the rank of Junior Bombardier and assuming the role of troop commander during our pass off parade—a momentous occasion marking the culmination of our training.

Life at Bramcote was hard, similar to the realities depicted in films such as "Full Metal Jacket."

Our only reprieve from the rigours of military life came in the form of fleeting moments, such as gathering around the television to watch "The A Team" on Saturday evenings—a brief, "Time-Out" from the demands of our training.

The fleeting respite of, "Chill Time," was abruptly interrupted by the arrival of our ever-vigilant Troop

Sergeant, bearing boxes of SLR magazines and live 7.62 mm rounds. As we lounged in front of the television, basking in the temporary reprieve from military duties, we were swiftly reminded of the ongoing demands of our training.

With a no-nonsense demeanour, our Troop Sergeant instructed us to practice loading 20, 7.62 mm rounds into a magazine, turning what was supposed to be a moment of relaxation into a multi-tasking exercise. Amidst the clatter of ammunition and the occasional mutter from our Sergeant, we found ourselves seamlessly blending the mundane with the surreal.

The lessons learned and bonds forged during those twelve months would serve as a guiding light throughout my military career, instilling within me a deep sense of duty and discipline.

As I reflect on my journey from army cadet to regular soldier, I am reminded of the invaluable role that Bramcote played. Though the path was arduous and filled with challenges, it supplied me with the foundations for my journey of service and self-discovery.

Sailing the Channel:

....

British soldiers do adventure training to build important skills and improve their overall fitness.

Activities like skiing, climbing, sailing, hiking and kayaking help them develop teamwork, leadership and problem-solving abilities.

It also pushes them out of their comfort zones, helping them stay mentally tough and physically fit, which is important for their roles in challenging and unpredictable situations. Plus, it gives them a break from regular military routines and boosts morale.

....

As a Junior Soldier, there are countless memorable moments that shape one's experience and leave an indelible mark on the journey of growth and self-discovery. Among these moments, one stands out as a truly unforgettable adventure: sailing the Channel on a yacht. It was an opportunity of a lifetime.

Sailing the Channel was far more than just a leisurely activity. It carried a profound sense of purpose and reverence. It became an expedition steeped in historical significance.

Selected for this unique voyage, I embarked on the yacht with a mix of anticipation and trepidation. The prospect of sailing across the Channel was exhilarating, yet the realisation that there was no onboard toilet presented a daunting challenge. It's hard not to chuckle at the memory now, but at the time, the absence of such basic amenities posed a practical concern that demanded creative solutions.

Setting sail from Southampton, the thrill of being "abroad" for the first time mingled with the sense of adventure that permeated the air. The sea stretched endlessly before us; a vast expanse of blue dotted with promise and possibility. As we navigated the waters towards Calais, I found myself immersed in the rhythm of the ocean.

Of course, the lack of a traditional toilet onboard proved to be a source of amusement and, admittedly, mild discomfort. The necessity of leaning over the edge for a bathroom break became a running joke among the crew. And yes, the inevitable question of what to do in case of a number two did cross our minds, I will leave that to your imagination.

Despite the unconventional facilities (or lack thereof), sailing the Channel stays one of the most cherished memories of my time as a Junior Soldier. It wasn't about the destination, but the journey itself.

A Boy Soldier's Journey: Reflections on Remembrance

As a boy soldier sailing the channel in a yacht, the experience seemed like a dream—a fleeting moment of respite amidst the rigours of military training. Yet, it was the poignant encounters with history during Operation Overlord that left an indelible mark on my young mind.

As we embarked on a poignant journey to visit the beaches where we and our allies landed on D-Day, we were acutely aware of the historical significance embedded in each stretch of sand.

Along the 50-mile expanse of the Normandy coast, the names Utah, Omaha, Gold, Juno and Sword resonated with the weight of sacrifice and heroism.

These were not just code names, but symbols of courage and determination, marking the sites where countless soldiers stormed ashore to turn the tide of World War II.

With each beach we visited, we paid homage to the bravery of those who faced unimaginable odds and forged a path to victory amidst the chaos of war.

The first thirty minutes of "Saving Private Ryan" offers a visceral and realistic portrayal of the harrowing experience of landing on the beaches of Normandy on D-Day. The film's meticulous attention to detail, from the chaotic and relentless gunfire to the sheer brutality of combat, immerses viewers in the intensity and terror of the battlefield.

The cinematography, coupled with the gritty realism of the set design and special effects, creates a sense of immediacy that is both gripping and haunting. Through its unflinching depiction of the horrors of war, "Saving Private Ryan" offers a powerful tribute to the bravery and sacrifice of the soldiers who fought and died on that fateful day.

It was a humbling experience that reaffirmed the enduring legacy of the greatest generation, and the debt of gratitude owed to those who fought and fell on the shores of Normandy.

Visiting the rows upon rows of gravestones in Bayeux War Cemetery in Normandy was a solemn and humbling experience. As I walked among the meticulously kept gravesites.

The sheer scale of the cemetery served as a stark reminder of the staggering human cost of war.

Each, three thousand eight hundred and six British and Commonwealth war graves bore the regimental number, name, regiment, date killed in action (KIA) and age of the brave soldier who had laid down their life in service to their country, while three hundred and thirty-eight gravestones have, "A Soldier of the Second World War" followed by a cross with the words, "Known unto God" chiselled into the white Lasa marble served as poignant reminder of the countless lives lost to the ravages of war.

The memories of those sacred grounds, where the echoes of history reverberate with haunting poignancy, remain etched in my memory to this day. The solemnity of Remembrance Sunday, with its sombre rituals and solemn tributes, serves as a poignant reminder of the debt of gratitude owed to those who made the ultimate sacrifice.

The Exhortation

The words recited on Remembrance Day encapsulate the enduring legacy of those who served:

" They shall grow not old, as we that are left grow old: Age shall not weary them, nor the years condemn.

For they were young, as we are young, and they served, giving freely of themselves. To them, we pledge, amid the winds of time, to carry their torch and never forget.

We will remember them."

These poignant words, spoken amid the solemn hush of remembrance, serve as a solemn vow to carry the torch of their memory forward, to honour their sacrifice, and to ensure that their legacy is never forgotten.

From Bramcote to Andermatt: My Skiing Adventure

My journey as a soldier took an unexpected turn once, I completed my training at Bramcote. Selected for a unique opportunity to learn how to ski and tackle challenging courses, after a long drive in a military Land Rover painted blue, we arrived in the picturesque village of Andermatt in Switzerland. It was a breathtakingly beautiful place; unlike anything I had ever seen before.

Upon arrival, we were given a couple of days to settle in before our intensive training began. For the next six weeks, six days a week, we were immersed in ski lessons led by a seasoned Swiss Olympic ski instructor. The experience was both exhilarating and gruelling as we pushed ourselves to master the fundamentals of skiing.

During the first two weeks, we tackled the basics without the aid of chairlifts, resorting to the classic method of skiing down and walking up. The effort required left our legs feeling like tree trunks, but the sense of accomplishment with each successful run made it all worthwhile. I found myself falling in love with the sport, relishing every moment spent on the slopes.

By the end of the six-week training period, thanks to the army's support, I had transformed from a complete novice into an, "okay" skier. The culmination of our training came with the opportunity to take part in the 3 Divisional ski championships; a chance I never imagined would come my way. Though I didn't qualify to race at the army championship, the experience was nothing short of exhilarating.

This stroke of luck marked the beginning of even greater skiing adventures for me. Despite not making it to the army championship, the memories and skills gained during those weeks in Andermatt served as a solid foundation for future skiing endeavours. It was a testament to the unexpected opportunities that can arise in the life of a soldier, each experience shaping and enriching the journey in its own unique way.

Chapter 5

Germany - BAOR (British Army of the Rhine)

From Snowy Slopes to Foreign Fields: My Journey to Germany - 1986

Embarking on a new chapter of life can often be a blend of excitement and apprehension, especially when it involves venturing into the unknown. My transition from the picturesque snowy slopes of Switzerland to the unfamiliar terrain of Germany marked the beginning of an unforgettable journey, both professionally and personally.

Having just bid farewell to the breath-taking landscapes of Switzerland, where I had indulged in exhilarating adventures on the slopes, I found myself standing at the threshold of a new experience. My destination: Münster, Germany, where I was to serve with 2nd Field Regiment Royal Artillery.

As a young recruit, this posting held the promise of challenges and opportunities I had never experienced., The journey started from Brize Norton, where the anticipation in the air was palpable. Touching down at RAF Gütersloh, Germany marked the first tangible step into this foreign territory. From there, a small minibus awaited, destined to transport three of us raw recruits to Münster.

As we embarked on this leg of the journey, a noticeable silence enveloped us, each of us lost in our own thoughts, contemplating the unknown path that lay ahead.

The landscape that greeted us as we traversed through the German countryside was a stark contrast to the snow-capped mountains of Switzerland. Fields adorned with vibrant yellow rapeseed stretched out before us, painting a surreal picture that symbolised the beginning of a new chapter in our lives.

Arriving in Münster, we were greeted by the bustling activity of military life, a stark contrast to the serene tranquillity of the Swiss Alps. The barracks became our new home, and as we settled into our routines, we began to navigate the intricacies of military service in a foreign land. A stark reminder that we were stationed in West Germany came with a directive, "not to fraternise with the local population." This instruction, while understandable given the geopolitical tensions of the time, served as a sobering reminder of the division that still existed between East and West.

Looking back on that surreal moment of arrival, I realise now that it was merely the prelude to a journey filled with growth, camaraderie, and resilience. Germany became more than just a posting; it became a crucible where bonds were forged, skills were honed, and memories were made that would last a lifetime.

Little did I know at the time that Germany would become my permanent residence up until now. It was in Germany that I found love and built a family.

1986 stands out as a pivotal moment marking the beginning of the end of the Cold War era. * The tensions that had gripped the world for decades began to thaw as diplomatic efforts and momentous events unfolded.

*Cold War era - 1947 – 1991

My early years serving Queen and country

Our living quarters, though cramped and often crowded, became a sanctuary amidst the rigours of military life. Sharing a room with three others presented its challenges.

The heart of our existence revolved around our weaponry, particularly the fearsome M109 self-propelled howitzers. These formidable machines symbolised not just our firepower but also our readiness to defend our nations interests at a moment's notice.

Yet, amidst the discipline and rigour of military life, there were fleeting moments of respite and recreation. Our camp boasted amenities such as a NAAFI (Navy Army and Air Force Institutes), cinema, cookhouse and a gym, providing brief respites from the demands of our duties.

Despite engaging in on-and-off relationships with girls back in England, none of them ever blossomed into something substantial. The constant factor in these failed romances was the inevitable distance imposed by my military service.

Chapter 6

Northern Ireland

Preparing for my first Operational Tour

The looming prospect of a deployment to Northern Ireland cast a shadow over our daily routines, driving us to intensify our training efforts in preparation for the challenges ahead. The months leading up to our departure were marked by a relentless regime of physical and tactical training, each session pushing us to our limits and beyond. From gruelling patrols to meticulous person and vehicle searches.

Fitness became a paramount focus, with hours dedicated to honing our physical endurance and stamina, recognising the vital role it played in our ability to execute our duties effectively.

Among the multitude of training exercises, mastering our shooting skills stood as a cornerstone of our preparation. Armed with the cumbersome 7.62 mm Self Loading Rifle (SLR), we devoted countless hours to the range, refining our marksmanship principals and ensuring that our proficiency with the weapon was second to none. Zeroing in on targets became second nature.

In addition to weapon ability, we underwent specialised training to address the unique challenges posed by the threat of improvised explosive devices (IEDs). A fortnight course conducted at Normandy Barracks in Sennelager offered invaluable insights into identifying and neutralising these deadly devices. Through hands-on exercises and classroom instruction, we gained the knowledge and skills necessary to detect and reduce the dangers posed by IEDs, a critical component of our mission readiness.

Crowd control training was a harrowing yet essential part of our preparation for deployment. Each of us was tasked with standing firm behind a six-foot Perspex/Hardened Plastic Riot shield, a symbol of our defence against the chaos of civil unrest. Under the watchful eye of instructors, we braced ourselves as a petrol bomb was hurled at our feet, unleashing a sudden explosion of flames that engulfed our shield and threatened to consume us. Despite the instinct to panic, we were trained to hold the line, to remain resolute in the face of danger. As the flames licked at our legs, our comrades rushed to our aid, swiftly extinguishing the fire with well-practiced precision. In that crucible of adversity, we learned not only the importance of discipline and teamwork but also the profound courage needed to confront the volatile realities of crowd control in conflict zones.

The intensity of our training was matched only by the gravity of the task at hand. Deploying to Northern Ireland meant confronting the realities of conflict requiring us to be not only physically prepared but also mentally resilient. Each day brought us closer to our departure date, heightening both anticipation and apprehension as we braced ourselves for the unknown challenges that lay ahead.

Northern Ireland -1987

My time in Northern Ireland stays a pivotal chapter in my life, marked by uncertainty, vigilance, and a sense of duty.

At the tender age of 19, I was thrust into the heart of a complex and volatile conflict, patrolling the streets of Bandit Country in South Armagh and standing guard at the imposing Maze Prison in County Down. As a young soldier, I was driven by a mixture of enthusiasm and naivety, propelled by a deep-seated love for my country and a fervent commitment to serving in the army. Yet, amidst the rugged beauty of the Irish landscape, I grappled with the harsh realities of my surroundings, often without a full understanding of the intricate political and historical forces at play.

Our days were filled with the gruelling routine of long patrols and Vehicle Check Points (VCPs) punctuated by the ever-present threat of violence lurking around every corner. Armed with the formidable 7.62 calibre SLR (Self Loading Rifle), we stayed on high alert, knowing that the slightest lapse in vigilance could have dire consequences.

Despite the hardships and the constant spectre of danger, I consider myself fortunate that no one from my troop suffered serious injuries during our time in Northern Ireland.

Looking back, those years shaped me in profound ways, instilling in me a deep respect for the sacrifices made by those who served alongside me and a sobering awareness of the complexities of conflict and its enduring impact on individuals and communities. Though the memories may fade with time, the lessons learned during my time in Northern Ireland will forever remain etched in my heart and mind.

Two weeks Leave

Upon my return from Northern Ireland, my Regiment graciously granted us two weeks leave, a respite eagerly embraced after the relentless pace of our deployment.

My journey home began with a complimentary flight aboard a C-130 Hercules to RAF Brize Norton, a ride that was as memorable for its roaring engines as it was for the anticipation of relaxation that awaited me. From there, I was given a train warrant to Looe, Cornwall, compliments of the Ministry of Defence (MOD) where a family reunion unfolded in the serene setting of a caravan park. My parents and sister were already there, basking in the leisure of holiday bliss, making it the perfect place to unwind. For the first time in months, I relished the luxury of not having to look over my shoulder, of walking freely with the confidence that comes from being in a "safe environment".

With money in my pocket from months of diligent service and a physique honed by the rigours of military life, I felt an exhilarating sense of invincibility. Those two weeks were a precious interlude of joy, a time to recharge and revel in the simple pleasures of family and freedom before the call of duty beckoned once more.

Chapter 7

Military Blood running through my veins

Lance Bombardier/Canada

Returning to barracks after a memorable time in Looe marked a turning point in my military journey, as I found myself selected to attend a rigorous six-week leadership course. As the youngest Gunner on the course, I was keenly aware of the weight of expectation and the opportunity it presented to prove myself.

At that point in my military career, my identity was deeply intertwined with my service; every aspiration and action revolved around the military. Surpassing my own expectations, I found myself among the top two performers in the course, a feat that resulted in an instant promotion to Lance Bombardier. However, with the promotion came its own set of challenges, particularly as I found myself in a position of seniority over soldiers who had far more years of experience in the army than I did.

The culmination of my training and dedication was put to the test during my first exercise in Canada in May 1989. This exercise provided a physical demonstration of the power and precision of our weaponry, as we fired our 155mm High Explosive (HE) shells with such accuracy and efficiency. The ability to swiftly transition from firing to our front to firing to our rear within seconds displayed how important our roles as artillery soldiers.

Ski Instructor/Cyprus/Bombardier

Life after returning from Canada took on the characteristic twists and turns of a rollercoaster ride, with each new challenge and opportunity propelling me forward on an exhilarating journey. Eager to expand my skill set and further my military career, I embarked on the Joint Services Skiing Instructor (Alpine) course, a rigorous six-week, seven-days-a-week endeavour. The intensity of the training pushed me to my limits, but the satisfaction of mastering a new skill made every moment worthwhile.

Barely catching my breath, I was soon thrust into another demanding training package, this time in preparation for a six-month tour to Cyprus.

Patrolling the green line in Nicosia was a surreal experience, as though time had stood still amidst the echoes of past conflicts. Yet, amidst the tension and history, there were unexpected opportunities for adventure. One such opportunity arose when I was unexpectedly sent to the summit of Troodos, a towering mountain, to work at the ski resort for three months.

Teaching personnel from all 3 services how to ski against the breath-taking backdrop of Troodos was a highlight of my time in Cyprus, blending adrenaline-fuelled pursuits with moments of tranquillity and natural beauty.

A particularly memorable occasion occurred on Christmas Eve, as I found myself skiing down the slopes in the morning and swimming in the crystal-clear waters of the Mediterranean Sea in the afternoon. It was a poignant reminder of the diverse experiences and contrasts that military life can offer, from the frozen slopes of the mountains to the sun-kissed shores of the coast.

Upon my return from Cyprus, I once again found myself selected to attend my second leadership course, a testament to my dedication and competence as a soldier. The six-week course proved to be both physically and mentally challenging, pushing me to my limits once again. Yet, through perseverance and determination, I appeared among the top performers, earning an instant promotion to Bombardier.

Special Forces

The decision to push myself further in my army career marked a significant turning point, fuelled by an insatiable desire to excel, and become the best of the best.

Contemplating joining elite units such as the Royal Artillery Commandos or the Special Air Service (SAS), I expressed my intentions to my Battery Training Officer, who took proactive steps to support my aspirations. His application for me to attend the Battlefield Survival Course, conducted by the SAS in Ravensburg, South Germany, near the Swiss border, opened the door to a transformative experience.

As a Bombardier I was the lowest rank and the youngest on the course, there was a mixture of SNCOs and Officers.

Despite this, I embraced the challenges with passion, immersing myself in the rigorous training regime focusing on survival skills and operating in hostile environments. From learning to live off the land to navigating through treacherous terrain, every aspect of the course resonated with my passion for excellence. The pinnacle of the course was the Escape and Evasion exercise, a simulation of evading capture in real-world scenarios.

The sudden intrusion of our living quarters by Special Forces personnel accompanied by German Alsatian attack dogs sent a surge of adrenaline and fear coursing through my veins. Captured, blindfolded and bundled into a vehicle, the sense of panic was visible as uncertainty loomed over the impending challenges.

Stripped of our possessions and given minimal resources, (two left boots!) the next days tested our resilience and resourcefulness as we evaded capture while being pursued by members of the Parachute Regiment.

Paired with an Intelligence Captain whose map reading skills were unparalleled, we navigated through the wilderness, relying on our wits and instincts to outmanoeuvre our pursuers.

The culmination of the exercise brought us to a critical point as we raced against time to rendezvous with a helicopter for extraction. With a raging river separating us from the Landing Zone (LZ), the sound of the approaching helicopter spurred us into action. Making a daring dash and swim for the LZ, we narrowly evaded capture and secured our place onboard the helicopter.

Detachment Commanders course (Bergen-Hohne Garrison).

The Battlefield Survival course tested my resilience in the face of adversity, and paving the way for further opportunities for growth and advancement within the military. Following this transformative experience, I was selected to attend a Detachment Commanders course at Hohne camp.

Spanning eight weeks, the Detachment Commanders course was an intensive and academically challenging program designed to prepare individuals like me to take on the role of Gun Number 1.

As a Gun Number 1, my responsibilities included routine inspections, servicing and helping REME (Royal Electrical and Mechanical Engineers) when something went, “Tits Up”. Also ensuring that all components listed in the Complete Equipment Schedule (CES). Layman’s terms “A massive toolbox was in serviceable and working order.”

My primary responsibility as a Gun Number 1 during live firing exercises was to ensure the safety and well-being of my crew of six, while also executing the fundamental task at the core of my role: firing a 45-kilogram High Explosive shell with precision and accuracy over distances of up to 24 kilometres. With meticulous attention to detail and rigorous adherence to safety protocols, I approached each firing exercise with the utmost care and professionalism.

Throughout the course, I faced many academic challenges as I grappled with the complexities of artillery operations and command responsibilities. However, fuelled by determination and a desire to excel, I persevered and passed the course with flying colours.

Upon completion of the Detachment Commanders course, I was entrusted with my own gun, B Sub, at the age of 24. This was a momentous occasion, one that I had not expected witnessing so early in my military career.

Taking command of my own gun stood for a culmination of years of dedication, training, and hard work, and symbolised a new chapter in my journey as a military leader.

Chapter 8

Saddam Hussein

Unexpected Turn

The trajectory of my military career took an unexpected turn with the invasion of Kuwait by Saddam Hussein in 1990, which brought my aspirations within the Special Forces to an abrupt halt. As tensions escalated and the need for swift and decisive action became paramount, the more senior Gun Number 1s within my unit were swiftly deployed to take part in the liberation of Kuwait.

I found myself held in reserve, poised on standby in case the situation escalated to a point where more reinforcements were needed.

The sudden halt to my special forces aspirations was a bitter pill to swallow, as I had invested considerable time and effort into preparing myself for the challenges and demands of such elite units.

The prospect of being relegated to a reserve role, while necessary from a strategic standpoint, was disheartening, leaving me grappling with feelings of frustration and disappointment.

However, as events unfolded and the situation in the Gulf region intensified, it became increasingly clear that my role as a reserve asset was vital in ensuring readiness and flexibility in response to evolving circumstances.

Although I didn't deploy to Kuwait initially, my opportunity came with Operation Granby* in March 1991, where I served as an expert in Artillery Munitions.

Stepping foot onto the scorched desert terrain, I was immediately greeted by the stomach wrenching scent of burning oil and the ominous sight of a black cloud hanging overhead.

The sweltering heat of the afternoon sun only intensified the gravity of the situation. Over the next five months, I assumed the role of second-in-command to a seasoned Sergeant, who served as an Ammunition Technical Officer (ATO). Our mission: to identify and destroy thousands of tons of unused munitions left behind in the wake of conflict. Recognising the enormity of the task at hand, I was entrusted with leading a team of twelve soldiers from various artillery regiments, pooling our expertise and resources to tackle this harrowing and daunting endeavour head-on.

*Operation Granby was the code name given to the British military operations during the 1991 Gulf War.

Stark Contrast

Returning to Münster from the sweltering hot desert of Kuwait was a journey marked not just by physical distance but also by a profound shift in environment and culture. Having spent time in a war zone, where vigilance and caution were constant companions, the transition to the calm and serene atmosphere of a plane flight seemed surreal. As I boarded the plane, leaving behind the harsh realities of conflict, I couldn't help but reflect on the stark differences in culture and lifestyle between these two worlds.

In Kuwait, the scorching heat and arid landscape served as a constant reminder of the harsh conditions endured by those living and working in the region.

In stark contrast, the atmosphere inside the plane was one of tranquillity and orderliness. The hum of conversation, the occasional laughter, and the gentle murmur of the aircraft's engines created a sense of calm amidst the chaos of the outside world.

As the plane soared above the clouds, leaving behind the desolate landscape of the desert below, I found myself immersed in a world of comfort and luxury that stood in stark contrast to the harsh realities of my recent experiences. Flight attendants moved gracefully through the cabin, offering refreshments and assistance with a smile.

Business as usual

Returning from a country ravaged by war is an experience that defies explanation. It's disorienting to see the stark contrast between the devastation left behind and the appearance of, "business as usual" in the world I return to.

As I walk down familiar streets, surrounded by people going about their daily routines, it's difficult to reconcile the scenes of destruction and hardship I've seen with the peace and, "normality" that characterise life we call home.

The sight of fully stocked shops and bustling markets, brimming with goods and necessities, stands in stark contrast to the scarcity and deprivation endured by those in war-torn regions. It's a reminder of the privilege and fortune that many of us take for granted.

Who would ever have thought I would be in Basra, Iraq, 12 years later stood in an Iraqi police station when news broke that Saddam Hussein had been captured in a spider hole near a farmhouse in Ad Dawr, near his hometown of Tikrit.

Chapter 9 –

Husband/Dad

Gunnery Instructor

The invasion of Kuwait in 1990 acted as a significant turning point in my life, abruptly halting my aspirations of pursuing a career in special forces. However, it was not just, Kuwait that influenced my decisions; life's intricate meandering twists and turns played its part as well.

Despite the challenges posed by my altered career trajectory, I found myself embracing the joys of life, relishing in activities like ski teaching and cultivating a social life that had previously been elusive due to my demanding schedule.

It was during the summer of 1991, in a beer garden overlooking the Aasee, a vast lake in Münster that I encountered a pivotal moment that would alter the course of my life

Little did I know that chance encounter would lead me to meet my future wife, who at that time was in her eighth year of a law degree, an amazing person, so good looking, super tall, with whom I would embark on a journey of love and companionship that would endure for 33 years and counting. Our relationship blossomed, growing stronger with each passing day, until it was put to the test by the demands of my posting to 17 Training Regiment and Depot, Woolwich, London.

As a gunnery instructor tasked with passing on my knowledge to recruits on the intricacies of the L118 Light Gun, I found myself immersed in a world of constant vigilance and responsibility.

Living in the same block as the recruits, I was on call 24 hours a day, facing the challenges of maintaining discipline and order amidst the chaos of military life. The barracks became a battleground in many ways, with conflicts erupting at any given moment. I vividly recall one harrowing incident where I intervened to prevent a recruit from stabbing another.

Despite the strains of a long-distance relationship, my love for my future wife only deepened with each passing day. Our fleeting moments together, whenever our schedules allowed, served as a beacon of hope amidst the rigours of military life. It was during these stolen moments that I realised the depth of my feelings, the undeniable truth that I was falling irrevocably in love.

As time flew by, filled with the relentless pace of military duties and the trials of maintaining a long-distance relationship, my love for my future wife remained unwavering. Each challenge we faced together only served to strengthen our bond, reinforcing the resilience and enduring nature of our love. And so, as I reflect on the journey that brought me to this moment, I am filled with gratitude for the twists and turns of fate that led me to her. In a world fraught with uncertainty, our love is still a steadfast anchor, guiding us through life's tumultuous seas with unwavering resolve and boundless devotion.

Will you marry me?

After mustering up the courage, I finally asked her to marry me, and fate had it that the proposal occurred in an unexpected place—an elevator at Heathrow Airport.

Armed with a diamond ring clustered with a striking red emerald at its centre, I nervously popped the question, and to my delight, she said yes. However, the joy was soon overshadowed by a twist of fate when, just a few months later, she managed to lose the precious ring. Nevertheless, our commitment to each other remained unwavering, and on March 19, 1993, we exchanged vows at her birthplace in Germany, a date forever etched in my memory as it coincides with my car's registration number!

Following our heartfelt union, we embarked on a dreamy honeymoon in the Caribbean, though not without its share of mishaps.

Nursing a fractured foot, I found myself spending most of our time together reclined on a beach chair. Adding a humorous anecdote to our wedding festivities, I attempted a flick-flak during the reception, only to misjudge my landing, much to the amusement of our guests.

Despite the setbacks, our love and laughter remained undiminished, and our bond grew stronger with each passing day. Yet, the reality of our transient military lifestyle soon brought us back to earth as duty called, separating us once again.

However, fortune favoured us when the army unexpectedly decided to cut short my posting in London, allowing me to reunite with my beloved wife in Germany.

With renewed hope and anticipation, I set my sights on our reunion, eager to embark on the next chapter of our adventure together in the land of beer, bratwurst, and boundless love.

I was posted to 26 (XXVI) Regiment Royal Artillery in Gütersloh as my old Regiment disbanded.

My wife's feedback

As I eagerly awaited my wife's feedback on the latest section of my book, her candid response to the "will you marry me" passage caught me off guard.

> With a hint of playful sarcasm, she remarked that it was "too soppy" and jokingly adding that it made her want to gag.

Her frank assessment served as a humorous reminder of her no-nonsense attitude and desire for keeping sentimentality in check. Despite her teasing critique, I couldn't help but appreciate her honesty and the light-hearted banter that characterised our relationship. With her unwavering support and witty commentary, she added a touch of authenticity to the writing process.

What is a Battery Reconnaissance Officer?

While reviewing the "Confidential Report" section of my unfinished book, a friend of mine casually posed a question: "What is a Battery Reconnaissance Officer?" (BRO). I immediately thought of the essential skills required for a BRO—particularly their expertise in map reading and their senior role within the Battery.

This prompted me to share with my friend the story of a significant incident from my past as a gunnery instructor at 17 Training Regiment Royal Artillery.

The Phase 2 Gunnery courses which we ran, were six intense weeks of both theory and hands-on experience with the L118 105mm Light Gun. Our aim was to transform phase 1 soldiers* into proficient gunners. The pinnacle of this training was a challenging five-day live firing exercise on Salisbury Plain, serving as a rigorous test for both instructors and recruits.

During a live firing exercise on Salisbury Plain, as was customary, our movement orders were issued by the BRO.

Equipped with nothing more than a map, compass and the trusty odometer which indicated distance I had travelled from our 1-tonne Land Rover.

My map reading skills were good, or so I thought. I plotted our new coordinates—15 km northeast from our current location—as the light rapidly faded, making navigation increasingly challenging I set off for our next gun position.

Approximately twenty minutes into our journey a command over the headset from zero (the Boss) to all call-signs shattered the silence: “STAND FAST.”

Once again, but in a more panicked voice, “Charlie Charlie 1** this is zero - STOP STOP STOP” followed by another fierce-toned “STAND FAST.”

Hearing the command over the radio sent shivers down my spine. I ordered my driver to stop immediately and turned to my six recruits to explain what had just unfolded. I could see the concern in their eyes, and I knew it was essential to share a similar experience to emphasise the gravity of the situation.

“Listen up everyone,” I began, making sure I had their full attention. “The only other time I have heard ‘stand fast ’ was during a live firing exercise in Canada.

We were conducting a “Danger Close” fire mission, firing artillery rounds extremely close to our own advancing troops. It’s a high-stakes situation where precision is critical.”

I could see my recruits hanging on my every word, fully understanding the seriousness of the scenario. I suddenly heard over the radio, “STOP STOP STOP, STAND FAST” It was a voice filled with urgency and alarm just as I had heard. One of my fellow gun number ones had made a massive mistake - he had inadvertently loaded and fired charge 4 instead of charge 5. This error meant that a 155mm high explosive shell fell short of the intended target.

Luckily, during that exercise, there were no casualties. But it was a stark reminder of how crucial it is to pay attention to every detail and follow procedures precisely.

Miscommunication or a simple mistake can have dire consequences.

Something BAD had happened, a death, a serious accident, or someone has seen something that could lead to severe injury or death.

"Charlie Charlie 1 this is zero" once again bellowed over the radio, "send location over". I replied, "Bravo two zero alpha, my location, Grid (six figures)".

Again, "Charlie Charlie 1 this is zero - Range control has eyes on a 1 tonne Land Rover towing a Light gun in the impact area***.

I knew that 17 Training Regiment (my Regiment) were the only exercising troops on Salisbury Plain that day, it could only be one of six-gun detachments. I knew it was not me. I knew where I was, and I knew I was not in the impact area!

The next command from Zero was new to me, Zero instructed all gun detachments to turn our main beam lights on when instructed to. "Bravo 1 zero alpha, main beam on", quickly followed by "lights off". "Bravo 2 zero alpha (my call sign) main beam on", a long pause followed by, "Bravo 2 zero alpha this is zero, get your backside out of the impact area and report to my location immediately."

Every time I watch the film "Top Gun" and hear the iconic scene where "Maverick" is instructed to get his "butt" above the hard deck and return to base, it reminds me of this story.

When I reported back, I was given the biggest dressing down of my career. My Commanding Officer was furious. I had made a serious mistake, and it could have led to severe consequences. Normally, such an error would result in a formal charge. This would have meant a disciplinary Regimental entry in my files and, worse, the loss of my chance to be awarded the Long Service and Good Conduct Medal.

My Commanding Officer decided to give me another chance. Instead of putting me on a charge, I was instructed to donate 500 pounds to a charity of my choice. Grateful for the second chance, I chose the NSPCC (National Society for the Prevention of Cruelty to Children). To this day, I'm not entirely sure why I picked that charity, but it felt like the right thing to do at the time.

I often wonder if my Battery Commander, who appointed me as the Battery Reconnaissance Officer one and a half decades later, knew about the time I accidentally drove into the impact area on Salisbury Plain. If he had known about that incident, would he still have trusted me with the key role of BRO? I think so!

It's quite ironic that my BRO course was held at Larkhill, on Salisbury Plain - the very place where I made my serious mistake years earlier. Luckily by then, we had

Global Positioning Systems. The introduction of GPS was a game changer, especially for me - I never got lost again!

So, the question looms - what went wrong? How did I end up in the impact area? To this day, I have no idea how I made such a grave error. The answer is obvious - my map reading skills that day were useless!

Something I have never disclosed until now is that I vividly remember jumping out of my 1 tonne Land Rover and opening a gate that had a sign saying, "NO ENTRY. LIVE FIRING IN PROGRESS." Writing this chapter of my book, I still can't believe I ignored that message. ("What a Plonker").

*Phase 1, also known as basic training, is the foundational stage where individuals embark on their journey to become soldiers. During this phase, recruits receive instruction on the fundamental principles of soldiering, including understanding the army's structure and operations, acquiring survival and fieldcraft skills, mastering first aid techniques and becoming proficient in rifle usage. Physical fitness is emphasised throughout Phase 1 training to ensure candidates are well-prepared for the demands of military service.

**Charlie Charlie 1 is a call sign used in the Armed Forces meaning "everyone".

***The impact area is an area with boundaries controlling where weapons, bombs etc can be fired or detonated.

A Battery Reconnaissance Officer in an AS90 Regiment plays a critical role in ensuring the effectiveness of artillery operations through detailed reconnaissance, accurate positioning, efficient communication and robust logistical support.

Sergeant/I'm a Dad

Returning to Germany, after my stint at Woolwich I was quickly promoted to Sergeant at a remarkably young age. However, the transition came with its own set of challenges, particularly navigating the rigid protocols and formalities of the Sergeants' Mess.

One memorable event that stands out is my first experience attending a Ladies' Dinner Night. Clad in Mess Dress, * I accompanied my wife, who was instructed to adhere to strict dress code guidelines, including wearing a dress below the ankle. The evening unfolded with a series of lengthy speeches that extended well into the night, with the enforced rule that no one, women included, could leave the table until the speeches concluded.

After the formalities, the "ladies" were asked to leave while the men remained behind to indulge in cigars and brandy, a tradition that underscored the hierarchical dynamics of the Warrant Officers' and Sergeants' Mess.

As time progressed, I witnessed a gradual relaxation of rules and regulations within the Mess, reflecting the evolving culture and attitudes of the military community.
*Mess Dress in a Royal Artillery Regiment refers to a special type of formal military uniform worn by Officers,

Senior Non-Commissioned Officers and in some regiments, Junior Non-Commissioned Officers, for formal events, dinners and ceremonies.

Unlike standard issue uniforms, Mess Dress is bought by individuals and is like a tuxedo but specifically designed with military traditions in mind. Featuring distinctive regimental colours and insignia and includes the wearing of miniature medals to reflect the wearer's service.

Bosnia was hitting all the headlines. The Situation Reports (Sit Reps) grew increasingly harrowing, serving as a stark reminder of the gravity of the impending deployment. Amid all the uncertainty and worry, my life took a major turn with the arrival of my son, bringing a profound and wonderfully life-changing shift to my world.

Eleven months prior to my scheduled six-month tour to Bosnia, my wife gave birth to our son, an event that filled me with indescribable joy and profound emotions. Suddenly, I found myself navigating the complex terrain of fatherhood, cherishing every moment spent with my new-born son. The impending deployment cast a shadow over our newfound happiness, forcing me to confront the realities of military service and the sacrifices it entails.

Despite the challenges and uncertainties that lay ahead, the love and bond shared with my wife and son served as a beacon of strength, guiding me through the trials and tribulations of military life. However just before deploying to Bosnia we had one last Official commitment to attend to.

Countess Mountbatten of Burma (Myanmar)

Prior to our Imminent deployment, as a young Sergeant, I had the honour of taking part in a remembrance parade that took place against the iconic backdrop of the white cliffs of Dover.

The event was distinguished by the presence of the Countess Mountbatten of Burma (Myanmar) as the inspecting officer. After three gruelling days of intensive drill instruction by a Colour Sergeant from the Coldstream Guards. The day unfolded with military precision, a seamless execution of duty and respect that could only be described as flawless.

While the officers had the privilege of hosting the countess, we the SNCOs found ourselves in a five-star hotel bar, having a well-deserved cold beer whilst enjoying the majestic view of the white cliffs of Dover.

Our Battery Sergeant Major (BSM). In a display of sudden resolve, slammed his pint glass on the bar, stood up with a commanding "Order", and decisively announced, "Gentlemen, follow me." Without hesitation, he led us out of the bar and towards the icy embrace of the sea. His next command was even more unexpected: "Gentlemen, strip."

Dressed in our No2 Dress uniforms and medals*, the scene that unfolded next was nothing short of surreal. In mere seconds, we were stripped bare, our hands instinctively cupping our private parts for warmth. Yet, the biting cold was so intense that you'd need a spyglass just to catch a glimpse. What followed was a moment straight out of a Monty Python sketch - ten hairy arsed fully grown men sprinting into the sea under the glow of a full moon.

The absurdity of the situation, coupled with the exhilarating rush of freezing water, transformed this into an unforgettable experience. This spontaneous act, a stark contrast to the disciplined precision of our earlier parade, underscored the unique bonds formed in the military.
*Number 2 Dress uniform is a traditional military uniform worn by soldiers and officers in the British Army. It's used for a variety of occasions, such as formal events, ceremonies and sometimes even for regular day-to-day duties.

Unlike Mess Dress this uniform is issued by the army, meaning that it's provided to soldiers and officers as part of their standard kit. The Number 2 Dress uniform includes a smart, khaki (yellowish brown) jacket and trousers.

One of the key features of this uniform is the display of medals. Any medals a soldier or officer has been awarded are worn on the left side of the jacket. In addition to medals, the uniform also clearly shows the rank of the person wearing it. For soldiers, their rank is displayed on the upper or lower arm, while officers have their rank shown on the epaulettes. This makes it easy to identify someone's position within the army just by looking at their uniform.

Chapter 10

Bosnia-Herzegovina - 1996

Bosnia-Herzegovina, a land haunted by the ghosts of conflict and division, holds a violent history that serves as a stark reminder of the depths of human suffering and resilience.

As a Sergeant and Commander of a self-propelled Howitzer known as an AS90, my deployment to Bosnia on an operational tour for six months thrust me into the heart of a landscape scarred by the ravages of war.

Bosnia marked a significant milestone in my military career, as it was my first operational tour as both a husband and a father.

Unlike previous deployments, where my concerns centred primarily on my own safety, this time my thoughts were consumed by the well-being of my family. (Even though my wife was capable on her own). However, the weight of responsibility bore heavily on my shoulders as I grappled with the realisation that my absence meant my wife bore the sole burden of raising our son while juggling a full-time job—a feat that demanded immense strength.

In an era before the "mobile phone," communication with loved ones was a challenge unto itself. The distant echo of Star Trek's futuristic technology seemed light-years away as the only means of connection was through a

Dictaphone leaving me yearning for the sound of my son's laughter and missing precious milestones.

As days turned into weeks and weeks into months, the absence of real-time communication underscored the stark reality of being separated from my family during such pivotal moments. The ache of missing my son's first steps cut deep, a poignant reminder of the sacrifices inherent in military service.

Despite the distance and the challenges of deployment, the unwavering bond shared with my family served as a source of strength and solace amidst the chaos of conflict.

Arriving as the first foreign troops on the ground, I bore witness to scenes that defied belief and tested the limits of human compassion.

The scars of conflict were etched into the very fabric of the land, manifesting in the shattered remnants of once-thriving communities and the eerie abandoned homes. Amidst the rubble and ruins, I encountered the harrowing tales of individuals torn apart by the brutalities of war, their lives forever altered by the indiscriminate fury of violence.

One of the most unforgettable sights were the mass graves scattered across the countryside, silent witnesses to the atrocities committed in the name of ethnic hatred and political ambition.

But perhaps even more shocking than the physical destruction was the visible sense of division and distrust that lingered in the air.

As I navigated the treacherous terrain of Bosnia, I felt a profound sense of disbelief and despair. How could humanity inflict such unspeakable horrors upon itself? How could we allow fear and hatred to triumph over empathy and compassion?

I did notice some glimmers of hope – from the tireless efforts of humanitarian organisations to the quiet gestures of kindness extended by ordinary citizens, I saw first-hand the transformative power of compassion and solidarity in the face of adversity.

My time in Bosnia left an indelible mark on my soul, a haunting reminder of the fragility of peace and the enduring legacy of war.

In the second chapter of my book, I delve into a deeply personal journey, marking the pivot away from my once steadfast belief in a higher power.

The catalyst for this profound shift was my operational tour in Bosnia, a period etched in my memory with vivid images of suffering, despair and the rawest forms of human pain.

Confronted daily with scenes that defied any notion of mercy or divine order, I found myself confronted with a haunting question: If a benevolent god truly presided over our world, how could such relentless suffering be allowed? This question, rooted in the harsh realities I saw, gradually eroded my faith, leading me to a place of scepticism and ultimately, rejection of the belief in a god who allows such atrocities to unfold under his watch.

Choosing Between Dreams and Duty

In the serene landscapes of Bosnia, under the shadow of my military duties, I found myself at an important crossroads, one that would irrevocably change the trajectory of my life and my family's future. It was during this period that I made two monumental decisions.

The first was to secure a future home for my family, a dream that seemed as distant as the peaceful life I yearned for. The second was a more profound internal battle, a choice between continuing my military career and prioritising my family's needs and aspirations.

Our dream home, a beacon of our future aspirations, stood elegantly around the corner from our military quarter.

My wife and I, often with our youngest son in tow, would pass by this house, allowing ourselves to dream of a life within its walls. The house represented more than just a physical structure; it symbolised stability, permanence, and a departure from the transient nature of military life.

Halfway through my tour, the universe seemed to conspire in our favour when a Dictaphone cassette from my wife announced that our dream house was for sale. This news, arriving amidst the chaos of military service, felt like a rare moment of sheer luck. Upon returning home for Rest

& Recuperation (R&R), we embraced the opportunity to be a family unburdened by the looming call of duty, and we secured our future by buying the house that had captured our hearts.

The decision to prioritise my family's well-being over my military career was fraught with complexity and contradiction. Military life, with its ethos of sacrifice and service, had been a source of pride and identity for me. Yet, the allure of domestic stability, the desire to see my children's growth, and the recognition of my wife's flourishing career painted a compelling picture of a different kind of life—one rooted in the home rather than in service.

This decision was unprecedented in my experience; choosing family life over a promising military career was not a path often taken by those in my profession.

Informing my superiors of my decision to prioritise family over the potential advancement to Warrant Officer, especially after being selected for the prestigious Gunnery Careers Course (GCC) in Larkhill, England, was met with surprise. This course, a gateway to significant promotion and recognition, represented everything I had worked towards in my career. Yet, the prospect of further absences from my family's daily life and the continuous uprooting of our lives for my career advancements loomed heavily over the potential accolades and promotions.

In an unexpected turn of events, my superiors opted for a "wait and see" approach. This decision allowed me to remain with my regiment, an unprecedented occurrence in a career defined by mobility and change.

Over the next 13 years, I served in various capacities, a testament to the adaptability and the toughness that are the hallmarks of military service. Yet, this extended period of stability within one regiment was a rare commodity that underscored the institution's recognition of the value of family and personal well-being.

The decisions made during my time in Bosnia were evidence of the broader struggles many service members face: the tug-of-war between duty and personal happiness, the quest for stability in a life of constant movement, and the deep-seated desire to be present for the milestones and everyday moments of family life. In choosing my family over the continuation of a rising military career, I embraced a path less travelled, affirming the irreplaceable value of time spent with loved ones and the pursuit of personal dreams. This journey, from the military quarters in Bosnia to the realisation of our dream home and a redefined sense of purpose, is a testament to the enduring strength of family bonds and the courage needed to pursue a life defined not by titles and accolades, but by love and presence.

Fish from Marillion

In the often unpredictable and charged atmosphere of military deployment, moments of levity and connection can appear in the most unexpected ways. My time in Sanski Most, Bosnia, serves as proof to this, blending the intensity of active service with the surreal experience of hosting a slice of home in the form of a concert. This particular tour, while demanding, afforded us some precious downtime, a brief respite from the responsibilities that come with serving in a conflict zone.

It was during one such interlude that the Army's Combined Services Entertainment (CSE) decided to grace us with a visit, bringing none other than Fish, the lead singer from Marillion, as the star attraction.

Tasked with the dual responsibilities of hosting our guests—an entourage of about twenty performers—and constructing a stage for the event, I found myself embroiled in a whirlwind of logistical challenges and excitement. The temporary accommodation prepared for our guests boasted a 1-star rating, yet it was a luxury compared to what we were accustomed to. The stage I had to build materialised into a structure that would not have looked out of place at Glastonbury, confirmation of the ingenuity and resourcefulness that military life demands.

With the two-beer rule firmly in place, anticipation built to a fever pitch as Fish took to the stage, greeted by an eruption of jubilant cheers from the packed-out makeshift stadium. The atmosphere was electric as he performed some of Marillion's biggest hits, including "Kayleigh" and "Lavender." It was a surreal moment, a slice of normality amidst the chaos of military operations.

The night took an unexpected turn when, after a few songs, Fish invited me on stage to express his gratitude.

Having already consumed my allocated two beers! I was in the spotlight, the focus of hundreds of pairs of eyes.

Fish's words of thanks were met with applause from the crowd; an overwhelming acknowledgment of the effort put into making the evening possible. Seizing the moment, I asked for the microphone, a decision fuelled by the euphoria of the night and, the liquid courage from my two beers!!!

What happened next has since become a moment of infamy in my personal history. With the microphone in hand, I launched into a rendition of "Chantilly Lace" by the Big Bopper, a personal favourite but starkly out of context in that moment. The audience's reaction was swift and unforgiving, with at least 200 empty beer cans flying in my direction amidst cries of confusion and booing. Fish's reaction, a simple "Mate, NOT COOL", was the epitaph to my brief ill-fated stage career, leading me to walk the walk of shame off the stage.

This incident, while embarrassing, has become a cherished story, a reminder of the camaraderie, the challenges, and the unexpected moments of levity that define military life. It speaks to the human need for connection, for a break from the norm, and the sometimes awkward, often endearing attempts to bridge the gap between the world at home and the realities of service abroad.

Even now, years later, the memory of that night, met with ridicule and laughter, stands as a testament to the unyielding determination of those who serve, finding humour and humanity in the most unlikely of places.

A Shit Story

During my time serving in Bosnia, amidst the solemnity and gravity of conflict, there emerged a story that my friends never get bored of, particularly during moments of light-hearted celebration- a tale that never fails to elicit laughter and amusement.

It was a bitterly wintry night as my troop of 3 AS90 SP Howitzers journeyed towards an area located approximately 10 kilometres West of Sanski Most. Traversing over snow-covered hills presented its own set of challenges, worsened by the urgent call of nature that suddenly struck me.

With a sense of urgency, I directed my driver to halt our AS90, and without a moment's hesitation, I leaped out of my hatch, clad in a cold weather parka with a fur-lined hood. Squatting by the side of one of the most powerful artillery weapon systems in the world, I hastily attended to my needs, it did not even touch the sides - it flew out like a rocket. Hastily pulling my parka over my shoulders and flipping my hood over my head to shield myself from the biting cold, we resumed our journey.

Returning to the comfort of my Number 1's hatch, I expressed my relief to my driver, commenting on the urgency of the situation and the satisfaction of finally finding relief. Yet, within moments, a pungent odour permeated the air, causing me to gag.

Confusion turned to frustration as I reprimanded my men, convinced that someone within the gun detachment had had a shit in the sanctity of our AS90.

It was only upon our deployment in a field that the truth dawned upon me - I had unwittingly shit in my parka hood during my urgent moment of need. My hair was covered in SHIT.

I had to wash my hair in a hostile environment, with freezing water, in a field, in the dark, freezing my tits off - the stench took days to eventually disappear.

For some reason, my German friends find that story much funnier than my English friends.

Chapter 11

Balancing Duty and Family

Returning from the arduous deployment in Bosnia, where the demands of duty often overshadowed personal priorities, I found solace and rejuvenation in the embrace of my family during a much needed two weeks leave. This period of respite offered not only an opportunity to reconnect with my loved ones but also a moment of reflection, prompting me to confront the delicate balance between military obligations and familial responsibilities.

Three months into my tour I had a conversation with my superior about the importance of placing family first had stirred within me a renewed sense of conviction. It was a sentiment that resonated deeply, yet its implementation seemed elusive amidst the rigours of military service. This changed when I was offered the role of Provost Sergeant.

Just over a year after returning from Bosnia, I was internally transferred to 55 The Residency Battery as the Provost Sergeant. In this role, I held significant responsibility for maintaining security, order and discipline within Mansergh Barracks.

Charged with overseeing the day-to-day operations of the security within the barracks and managing the regimental police force, I assumed a multifaceted role that demanded both vigilance and empathy.

Central to my duties as Provost Sergeant was the oversight of eight "prison cells", where soldiers serving sentences of no more than 14 days detention were housed.

When a soldier found themselves relegated to the confines of the detention centre, they entered what seemed like another world. Stripped of their freedom and subjected to the rigours of military prison life, detainees faced a harsh reality within four walls. Far from a recreational retreat, the detention centre served as a sobering reminder of the consequences of misconduct within the ranks, with little room for comfort or leniency.

As Provost Sergeant, my approach to overseeing the detainees was characterised by a firm yet fair demeanour. I kept a consistent standard of discipline and accountability. While I enforced the rules with unwavering resolve, I also ensured that fairness and justice prevailed in every interaction. This balance between firmness and fairness fostered an environment of respect and mutual understanding.

Monster

As a Provost Sergeant, I encountered many challenges, a couple incidents stand out vividly in my memory.

It was a Saturday evening when I received an urgent phone call informing me that the Military Police had apprehended a soldier from another camp for grievous bodily harm (GBH) in Gütersloh city centre, and they requested my presence. Upon arriving at the guardroom, I was greeted by the sight of two military police cars stationed outside - a stark sign of the severity of the situation.

The soldier in question, described as a towering six-foot-six figure and built like, "A Brick Shithouse" had proven to be a formidable challenge for the six military police officers who themselves were all over 6 foot!

As the detainee was carried handcuffed into his cell and he was released from his restraints his aggression manifested in relentless kicks against the reinforced metal door, posing a significant safety risk for both him and others.

Recognising the urgency of the situation, I made the decision to intervene, albeit with caution. However, attempts to open the door proved futile as the detainee's sheer strength had bent the metal frame, rendering it jammed shut. With no other option, I summoned the aid of a welder from the Royal Electrical and Mechanical Engineers (REME) to cut a hole using an oxygen acetylene cutting torch. A measure necessary to ensure the detainee's safety and restore order within the barracks.

Luckily as the door opened the soldier had calmed down. I went in, sat down on his bed as he stood towering over me and said, "Brew". He looked at me in total confusion as I replied, "Tea or Coffee". From then on, he was like putty in my hand that was until we had to transfer him to MCTC (Military Prison in Colchester). It took 6 soldiers to escort him when it should only take 2 - I will leave that story for another day. Never a dull moment!

Fire Alarm

Another story that to this day I tell my German friends repeatedly, while serving as Provost Sergeant, amidst the daily routines of keeping order and discipline within the barracks, there emerged moments of unexpected camaraderie and cross-cultural exchange.

One such memorable event unfolded when I received an invitation to visit the newly constructed German Police station in Gütersloh.

This invitation, a testament to the collaborative relationship between our regiment and the German Police, presented an opportunity for mutual understanding and shared experiences.

Arriving at the German Police station with a sense of anticipation and curiosity. Little did I know that this visit would culminate in an incident that would leave me red-faced with embarrassment.

Prior to my arrival, I was asked to bring along a couple of our side arms, the 9mm Browning pistols, as the German Police boasted an indoor range. I was presented with a choice between firing our Browning pistol or their Walther P99. Opting for the latter, I eagerly loaded my magazine, oblivious to the chain of events that would follow.

As I took aim and fired, the adrenaline coursing through my veins fuelled enthusiasm, leading to a rapid succession of shots that echoed through the range.

In the blink of an eye, I emptied my magazine, and to my annoyance, the shrill sound of the fire alarm pierced the air.

In that moment of embarrassment, amidst the blaring sirens and startled expressions, I found myself grappling with a mixture of amusement and mortification. I blame the person who cleaned the pistols - far too much gun oil!!!

I'm a Dad - Number 2

Becoming a father once more was a momentous occasion, etched in memory by the arrival of my youngest son on the 2nd of January 1998. Despite the anticipation of his imminent birth, life continued its course, marked by the obligations and duties inherent in military service.

On the evening of his arrival, I found myself attired in Mess dress, attending a function in the Sergeants 'Mess, when a fellow soldier urgently relayed the news of my wife going into labour. Maintaining composure amidst the flurry of emotions, I embarked on the journey home, adhering diligently to the speed limit!!!

Arriving home in a panic, still dressed in my Mess dress, I entered the scene of anticipation and excitement, looking to provide comfort and support to my wife during the pivotal moments of childbirth. During the whirlwind of emotions, I ensured the well-being of my elder son by arranging for his care with our neighbour, before turning my full attention to the miracle unfolding before me.

Hours later, in the same hospital my first son was born, my wife gave birth to our second son.

Babe and my two boys

For the past 33 years, I've had the privilege of sharing my life with my super cool, amazing wife, whom I still affectionately call "babe". Meeting her and bringing our two sons into this world stands as the pinnacle of my accomplishments. It's a chapter so rich and fulfilling that I could fill "ten books" with the stories and memories that define it.

From the moment our paths crossed, I knew I had found my soulmate, a partner whose love, support and unwavering presence have enriched every aspect of my existence. And then, becoming parents to our two incredible boys added an entirely new dimension to our lives, filled with laughter, challenges and boundless love.

I couldn't have wished for a more amazing partner or more wonderful children, and every day spent with them is a testament to the blessings that grace my life. They are the heart and soul of my journey, the foundation upon which my greatest joys and fondest memories are built.

Their existence and unwavering support have been the cornerstone of my resilience and recovery, a beacon of hope in moments of darkness.

Chapter 12

Down time

During my 15 years as a SNCO, there were two places that will forever be etched into my mind: The Warrant Officers' and Sergeants' Mess (The Mess) and "Fat Harry's" Bar.

The Mess held a special significance, serving as the hub of camaraderie and professionalism among peers. It was where bonds were forged, stories shared, and invaluable mentorship imparted.

On the other hand, "Fat Harry's" Bar, nestled in the comfort of my best mate's cellar, offered a different kind of sanctuary. Transformed into a German-themed haven, complete with a professional karaoke setup, it was the "place to be" for downtime bliss. There, amidst laughter and song, we found solace from the rigours of service, strengthening friendships that would endure a lifetime.

The Mess

The Warrant Officers' and Sergeants' Mess stood as an emblem of exclusivity, its membership not gained by wealth but earned through unwavering dedication and hard work. Throughout my 15 years as a Mess member, my wife and I never missed a single function. (Well maybe one or two).

The Mess was a fortress of tradition and celebration, hosting themed nights nearly every month, each one a testament to the wide-ranging tastes and vibrant spirit of its members. Ranging from Bavarian Nights to the whimsical charm of a, "Vicars and Tarts" night, there was always an occasion to let loose and embrace the camaraderie of service life.

The highlight of our calendar was undoubtedly the dinner nights, held approximately every two months, where we donned our Mess Dress and the ladies in their ball gowns, immersing ourselves in an evening of elegance and sophistication.

Entertainment at Dinner Nights was elevated to new heights with the presence of a military band. Their performances were nothing short of extraordinary, captivating audiences with their skill, precision and passion for music. Each note reverberated through the halls, stirring emotions and creating an atmosphere of awe and admiration.

Their repertoire ranged from stirring military marches to soulful ballads, ensuring there was something for everyone to enjoy. Their presence added an undeniable sense of grandeur and tradition to every function, making each performance an unforgettable experience etched into the memories of all who had the privilege of attending. However, it was the annual spectacles of the Christmas and Summer Balls that truly captured the essence of the Mess experience.

With extravagant buffets, minimum 5-piece bands flown in from the UK, and festivities that stretched into the early hours of the morning, these events were not merely social gatherings, but cherished traditions woven into the fabric of our military family.

As the night waned and the first light of dawn illuminated the horizon, the promise of a hearty English breakfast served as a fitting conclusion to a night filled with laughter, camaraderie and memories to last a lifetime.

The Warrant Officers' and Sergeants' Mess was more than just a venue; it was a sanctuary where bonds were forged, memories cherished, and the spirit of service celebrated in all its glory.

Fat Harry's Bar

The second place forever etched into my memory is Fat Harry's. Its name remains a mystery to me—to this day, I don't understand the "Fat" prefix, especially since Harry wasn't fat at all. But perhaps it's that touch of mystery and humour that added to its charm.

Unlike the Warrant Officers' and Sergeants' Mess, which was our exclusive club, Fat Harry's was the sanctuary for unbridled joy and relaxation. If we weren't at the Mess during the weekends, you could bet we'd be at Fat Harry's, engaging in the kind of partying that only such a unique spot could inspire.

There, against the backdrop of laughter, music and the clinking of glasses, we would talk nonsense and belt out songs on the Karaoke machine until the early hours of the morning.

However, Fat Harry's wasn't a place without order. There were rules, 10 of them to be precise, that added a layer of amusing governance to our escapades. Rule number 1, Harry is the Boss, set the tone, reminding us all whose domain we were in. Rule 2, "Only doubles to be served," ensured that the night would always be lively. Rule 3 reserved "Mack the Knife" exclusively for Harry's rendition, a testament to tradition and perhaps Harry's unique attachment to the song. The rules continued in this vein, each adding its own flavour to the bar's atmosphere and ethos.

But it was Rule number 10 that held a special place in our hearts, specifically targeting my wife with a humorous yet firm decree: "Under no circumstances are you to give Joe's wife the microphone after 2200hrs!" This rule, though playfully aimed, spoke volumes about the nights we had shared, the laughter that echoed off the walls, and the memories we made.

Fat Harry's was more than just a bar. It was a haven where ranks and formalities melted away, where friendships deepened, and where music and high spirits filled the air.

16 Battery (Sandham's Company)

The next couple of years marked a period of relative tranquillity compared to the whirlwind of activity I had experienced previously. Despite occasional stints away on live firing exercises, life settled into a steady rhythm, affording me the rare opportunity to prioritise family time.

……………………………………………

The following two paragraphs are from my Curriculum Vitae - "Translated into Civilian Talk."

Responsible for the smooth running of a Senior Managers' Social club, with over 160 members at a five-star standard. The club serves three meals a day and has a bar open seven days a week and is permanent accommodation for up-to 40 senior Managers

Responsible for the planning, finance and implementation of exclusive functions with over 250 customers within a set budget. This included a three-course meal, drinks and entertainment.

……………………………………………

This respite from the frantic pace of military life did not equate to idleness. I found myself immersed in a variety of roles, from serving as Rear Party Regimental Sergeant Major to managing the Sergeants' Mess, and later transitioning to the Officers' Mess upon promotion to Staff Sergeant.

In early 2003, a pivotal moment arose when I was approached by one of the Battery Commanders with a proposition to join 16 Battery in their deployment to Iraq as part of Operation Telic 3 *

……………………………………

*Operation Telic 3 was a phase of the British military's involvement in Iraq, specifically in the city of Basra, from November 2003 to April 2004. During this time, we (British forces) were focused on stabilising the region after the invasion of Iraq earlier in 2003. Our tasks included maintaining security, supporting the local government, and helping to rebuild infrastructure. It was part of the larger effort to help Iraq recover from the war and transition to a more stable and peaceful situation.

……………………………………

The invitation came at a poignant juncture, as one of my closest friends, a Warrant Officer in 16 Battery, was grappling with the devastating reality of his wife's battle with cancer, rendering him unable to deploy.

Though the Battery Commander's offer initially seemed like a polite gesture, it soon became clear that he was serious, and I found myself catapulted into a whirlwind of preparations for the impending deployment.

Undoubtedly, one of the most challenging aspects was breaking the news to my wife and children. The prospect of leaving them behind to embark on a mission fraught with uncertainty weighed heavily on my mind. As I embarked on the rigorous training regime in preparation for Operation Telic 3, I was acutely aware of the sacrifices that lay ahead, both for myself and for my loved ones.

Chapter 13

Iraq (BASRA) - 2003

My final Operational Tour

My final Operational Tour in Basra, Iraq, stands out as the most challenging chapter of my military career. My role was incredibly diverse, from working in the G5 cell to taking on the responsibilities of Operations Warrant Officer.

....

Extract taken from my Confidential Report - written by my Battery Commander.

"In addition, he has ably understudied the Operations Warrant Officer, during the last month of the tour, where he ably coordinated a series of complex operations against confirmed terrorist targets."

....

From the outset, we were confronted with an invisible enemy - improvised explosive devices (IEDs), shootings, and the complexities of navigating through diverse cultures and language barriers. Life within the "safe confines" of our base, housed within the old Ba'ath Party headquarters had its own challenges, from washing and shaving in a porter cabin while wearing our helmets. (The Iraqi people loved firing their weapons in the air, "Those bullets have to come back down to earth again"). It was extremely cold in winter and blisteringly hot in the summer months.

Each day, as I ventured beyond the "base's protection", (the base had been mortared on many occasions) the looming threat of IEDs weighed heavily on my mind. Despite the presence of armoured vehicles, the potential for serious harm from these explosive devices was ever-present, leading to constant apprehension that I might not return to base intact or alive.

This fear became all too real on one occasion when a patrol from my Battery were involved in a "Contact" situation, resulting in seven of our soldiers being flown to a makeshift British hospital with shrapnel wounds.

Visiting them first-hand was a poignant and unforgettable experience, serving as a stark reminder of the risks we faced daily. Additionally, we found ourselves entangled in riots, with my Battery making headlines across the UK as images of our soldiers engulfed in flames splashed across newspapers.

During my time in Basra, encountering scenes of executions became tragically commonplace, a grim reminder of the brutality of conflict. Something that worries me is, I cannot actually recall the exact number of times I stumbled upon executed former Ba'ath Party* members as they were left as gruesome displays for all to witness.

Ba'ath Party*

The Ba'ath Party in Iraq was a political organisation that ruled the country for many years, especially under the leadership of Saddam Hussein. The Ba'ath Party came to power in Iraq in 1968 and remained in control until 2003. Throughout this period, they governed the country with an iron grip, frequently using violence to suppress any opposition. Under Saddam Hussein's leadership, the party committed numerous human rights abuses, targeting various ethnic and religious groups, particularly the Kurds and Shia Muslims.

When Saddam's regime was toppled in 2003, a power vacuum emerged, and those who had been oppressed for so long were filled with anger. In places like Basra, this anger was directed at former Ba'ath Party members, who were viewed as collaborators in Saddam's brutal policies.

The execution and public display of these former Ba'athists were acts of retribution, intended to punish those responsible for so much suffering. These displays also sent a clear message: the old regime was gone, and any lingering support for the Ba'ath Party would not be tolerated. These actions were part of a broader cycle of violence and revenge that often follows the fall of oppressive regimes, where people seek justice for past wrongs, sometimes in brutal and very public ways.

One moment etched into my memory with chilling clarity is the sight of a man, his hands bound, lying motionless at a busy crossroads, a single bullet hole in his forehead, and the ominous label of "Ba'ath Party" pinned to his chest.

The streets bore witness to the silent horror of these executions, as blood congealed on the asphalt. Yet, among the haunting memories that haunt me to this day, there is one I vowed never to recount.

It was a day like any other in the perilous thoroughfare known as "IED alley." As we cautiously navigated the treacherous terrain, our eyes scanning for signs of danger, we came across a vehicle with its rear doors flung open. I approached with extreme caution and as I looked inside, I saw something that still to this day gives me nightmares. On the back seat a mother, father and their two sons (barely older than my two boys) hands bound, each with a single bullet hole to their foreheads and once again a tatty bit of paper with, "Ba'ath Party," written in bold type. (I cannot describe the scene in detail as words can never… you know the rest). All the while having a surreal feeling that the perpetrators have, "eyes on".

The memories of my time in Basra are etched deep within me, serving as a sobering reminder that some experiences cannot be erased or undone.

It wasn't until a couple of years later that I fully grasped the toll my deployment to Iraq had taken on my two boys. They confided in me, sharing their deep-seated fears and anxieties during those uncertain days, terrified at the thought that their dad might not come home. As a parent, it was a sobering realisation, that I was to blame for their pain.

Battery Commander:

16 Battery (Sandham's Company) Royal Artillery were deployed on OPERATION TELIC III - IRAQ, BASRA - November 2003 - April 2004.

Deployed as riflemen in the infantry role as part of the Royal Regiment of Wales Battle Group. Our area of responsibility (AOR) has incorporated well over a third of a city the size of Birmingham and included the infamous Shia Flats area where Saddam Hussein had relocated the Marsh Arabs having destroyed their natural habitat.

This has been an operational tour like no other. Over the past six months we have fielded over 2200 patrols into this most complex of urban environments, with Sandham's Company soldiers gaining the trust of the people through the combination of a disarming manner and hard professional edge.

We have pursued and closed with a shadowy enemy and through offensive operations removed the head of at least one terrorist organisation planning to impose the views through violence and intimidation. Through doing the basics of our profession well, we have discovered several explosive devices and disrupted them before they could harm the innocent. In addition, the opposite end of the broad operational spectrum we have spent in excess of $1.2 million, rebuilding and enhancing the infrastructure of a city disabled by 35 years of tyranny and neglect. Hundreds of children will now be educated in schools rebuild by Sandham's Company.

For my part, I am fiercely proud of the batteries conduct during such a unique, diverse and demanding operation.

The members of Sandham's Company will never forget some of the sensations they have experienced during the tour. We have witnessed the very best and the very worst of human nature. For many it has been a baptism of Fire, for others a combination of skills learnt long ago and refined over years of colour service. Regardless of rank or experience we have all been tested.

The Battery has achieved its mission and done so in the finest traditions of the Royal Regiment of Artillery. I could not have wished for what the Battery has accomplished, and I am honoured to have commanded Sandham's Company throughout Operation TELIC 3.

G5 Cell:

"A G5 cell is a unit or team responsible for civil-military cooperation. In a nutshell - they work on building and maintaining good relationships between the military and the local civilian population in areas where the army is operating".

Throughout the Operation TELIC 3 deployment the G5 Cell have dealt with an exciting and diverse range of challenges and responsibilities in post-war Basra.

The nature of our task has taken us to the furthest corners of our AOR on a daily basis to examine areas of concern, develop relationships with local tribal and religious leaders, or monitor projects that we have implemented.

We have been presented with many local infrastructure problems within the city and a large proportion of the essential services, namely water, electricity, solid waste removal and fuel distribution - either operate intermittently or have failed completely.

It has been a real challenge to continually find new and innovative solutions to these large-scale problems, and one that has seen us directly involved in directing resources at ministry level. The challenge is also extended to pacifying frustrated Iraqis who fail to understand that major repairs cannot be completed overnight!

We have instigated and managed over 30 projects intended to reinforce the local economy, security and the perception of Coalition Forces. Once underway close supervision and monitoring of the projects has been required, and we have spent a total of more than $1.2 million in our AOR.

This has included building new traffic calming schemes and bridges, undertaking the renovation of schools, police stations and the city fruit market, and erecting new street lighting in urban areas and fitting security measures at key sites such as electricity substations and water treatment plants.

Our role has been very gratifying during Operation TELIC 3 and has given both of us the opportunity to see almost every aspect of the tour. As well as being soldiers we have been builders, surveyors, water engineers, accountants, negotiators and petrol station managers. Flexibility and an open mind have been essential!

Contact - Wait Out

Throughout the tour, my roommate happened to be a Captain, and for the initial months, we were nearly inseparable, navigating the complexities of our mission together. In the fading light of dusk, my roommate and I found ourselves on a patrol, the tension palpable in the air. Suddenly, the crackle of the radio shattered the silence: My roommate ever so calmly sent a message to Zero Alpha - "Charley one zero alpha, contact wait out".

Bullets whizzed past us from the right flank, a chilling reminder of the imminent danger. With adrenaline coursing through our veins, we pressed forward, "advancing to contact," running towards the source of the gunfire. In that heart-pounding moment, I couldn't help but marvel at the surrealism of the situation, (I actually used the "F" word several times) only on day two of our deployment, and already thrust into the chaos of combat. Despite our efforts, several house searches yielded no results, leaving us grappling with the elusive nature of the hidden enemy lurking in the shadows.

The Weight of Responsibility: A Moral Dilemma

As a patrol commander tasked with ensuring the safety of my team on a routine mission, I found myself faced with a harrowing situation that would forever test my resolve and humanity. It was a seemingly ordinary day, enroute to a recently renovated school, when a chilling report over our communications system sent a shiver down my spine.

One of my soldiers, positioned as "Top cover", alerted me to the presence of an individual armed with an AK-47.

With a sinking feeling in my gut, I ordered the convoy to reverse so I could assess the situation first-hand.

As I dismounted, I was confronted by a scene that would remain etched in my memory for years. There, standing on the steps of a Mosque, was a young boy, barely older than my own sons. His small frame was tense with fear, and he clutched a weapon tightly to his chest. The sight was both shocking and heart breaking, as it was strictly forbidden for civilians to be on the streets with any sort of firearm. The gravity of the situation hit me hard, knowing that such a young child was caught in the throes of conflict, forced into a role far beyond his years.

Surrounded by a team of twelve highly trained soldiers and accompanied by a Royal Military Police Corporal. As we cautiously approached the boy, the tension in the air was palpable, every nerve on edge, every instinct screaming for caution. My Sergeant barked orders, demanding the boy lower his weapon, but all I could see in the boy's eyes was raw, unadulterated fear.

In that moment, amidst the chaos and confusion, I made a decision that would shape the course of events—and perhaps the course of my life. With my heart pounding in my chest, I ordered my patrol to silence, signalling for calm amidst the storm. Slipping my SA 80 rifle behind my back, (knowing I had my 9 mm browning pistol wedged between my body armour which was within arm's reach) I sought to defuse the volatile situation.

With my interpreter by my side, I implored the boy to lower his weapon, to recognise that he was outnumbered and outmatched. Yet, even as signs of compliance appeared, as he lowered his weapon to the ground, I could sense that something was about to take an unexpected turn.

And then, in a heart-stopping moment the boy raised his weapon once more, cocking it with a click that echoed through the narrow streets like a gunshot. As if orchestrated by a conductor twelve SA 80 assault rifles were cocked in unison sending a 5.56 mm high velocity round up the chamber and we were also supported with a couple of 5.56 light machine guns, the formidable "Minime" (which have the capability of firing 1000 rounds a minute) covering our rear. In that instant, with the weight of a boy's future heavy upon my shoulders, I faced a choice—do I succumb to the instinct of self-preservation, (shoot him) or should I heed my gut and walk away? Everyone knew that nearly every household harboured some sort of weapon. As I stared into his eyes, I could see the terror. He was just a boy in the wrong place at the wrong time. I hoped to God that my instincts were correct.

I was also fully aware that a single radio call to Zero would set the QRF (Quick Reaction Force) in motion, hurtling toward our location in a couple of armoured infantry fighting vehicles, the British Army's formidable, Warrior, armed with a 30mm RARDEN cannon and backed by a 7.62 chain gun, represented a force to be reckoned with. Yet, amidst the adrenaline and readiness, I remained mindful of the unpredictable nature of combat;

firefights could erupt suddenly but could also cease just as unexpectedly.

Calling the Quick Reaction Force would only escalate the situation further. While the instinct to respond swiftly and decisively is strong, it's crucial to weigh the potential consequences. Sometimes, restraint and strategic patience can be more effective in diffusing tensions and preventing further escalation in volatile situations.

A million scenarios were flashing through my mind. The road was narrow flanked with buildings - the houses provided, "the upper hand" to those wishing us harm if this were to go, "Pete Tong". In the end, I chose the latter, opting to walk away. It was a decision fraught with uncertainty and risk, but one that I knew, deep in my heart, was the right thing to do. As I reflect on that incident, I am reminded of the complex and often agonising choices that soldiers must make (sometimes in a split second) in conflict.

Finding Humour Amidst Adversity: Tales from Iraq

"Shit Container"

My deployment to Iraq presented countless challenges, but amidst the adversity, the power of humour, "Squaddie-Banter" lightens even the darkest moments. Two particular incidents stand out.

Anything to do with, "Shit" makes us squaddies laugh, whether, farting, throwing a "hand fart", (Farting in your hand and throwing it in your mate's face) stinking a room out or shitting in the hood of your Parka!!! - Even now I am asking, "Alexa" to make a fart sound!

Our portable toilets known as; "Thunderboxes" were dotted around camp. Picture this: locals armed with an industrial hoover attached to a massive metal container, dutifully emptying our "Thunderboxes". These seemingly harmless, "shit containers" had to be meticulously searched for IEDs as they entered our camp. Enter one of our fearless Superior Officers, who, in a display of true leadership (and perhaps a touch of madness), volunteered for the unenviable task of conducting the first search.

Now, if that's not a prime example of what we affectionately called a "Shit Job", I don't know what is! It was a moment of levity in an otherwise intense and serious environment, reminding us that even in the midst of chaos, there's always room for a good laugh.

"Sir, all due Respect - F……. O…."

My roommate (Who was a Captain and was senior to me) and I were conducting a routine patrol when we encountered a potential threat—an object that bore all the hallmarks of an Improvised Explosive Device (IED). As we lay there, assessing the situation with a pair of binoculars tension hung thick in the air.

In a moment that perfectly encapsulated the absurdity of our circumstances, my roommate turned to me and issued a directive: "You go forward and confirm if it's an IED or not." His words hung in the air, and for a moment I gave him a look of confusion. Summoning my own sense of humour amidst the gravity of the situation, I decided to respond with a touch of wit. “Sir,” I began, “are you married?” His response was quick and definitive, “You know I’m not.” Undeterred, I pressed on, “Sir, do you have any kids?” Again, he confirmed, “You know I have not got any kids.” If you are a member of the armed forces or a civilian, I STRONGLY recommend against attempting what you are about to read. Doing so could land you in serious trouble. With a playful grin, I delivered the punchline, “Sir, with all due respect, Fu…O… - YOU go and confirm if it’s an IED or not, if anything happens to me - you will be the one who must tell my wife and two boys, Sir.” The tension broke, replaced by the sound of laughter echoing through the air. In that moment, we found solace in humour, a brief respite from the harsh realities of our surroundings. In the midst of chaos and uncertainty, “Banter” became a potent weapon—a source of resilience and a testament to the invincible soldier's spirit. SO, was it an IED? We sought confirmation from a local bystander. With a casual manner, the individual approached the suspect device and, without hesitation, booted the suspect device. The resounding thud and lack of explosion gave the definitive answer we were after—it was not a bomb. In that simple act, the tension dissolved, replaced by a collective sense of relief.

Our mission brought us face to face with the grim reality of encountering uncomplicated yet lethal explosive devices. Despite their basic construction, these devices remained potent threats, in which their only intention was to seriously maim or kill.

Chapter 14

Homecoming/Cyprus

Following a Decompression* couple of days at RAF Akrotiri, Cyprus and a well-deserved two-week break, it was back to the routine of camp life.

*Decompression (DcN) must occur in a formal, structured and monitored environment, away from the area of operations immediately before recovery to the home base.

Here, personnel are provided with a location in which to rest, relax and reflect before returning to a normal, routine, home environment.

…………………

Direct quote from my Battery Commander:

"As Battery Training Officer he drove down the training requirements to return the Battery back to Gunnery. As Reconnaissance Officer, he proved his field ability during a live firing exercise. Without his personal input, the leadership course would not have happened."

…………………

My Regiment had deployed on Operation Tosca, Cyprus, leaving me behind to ensure the smooth running of the Rear Party and as my military contract approached its expiration after 24 years of service (including two served for free in the Junior Leaders Regiment Royal Artillery), I found myself at a crossroads, contemplating the next chapter of my life outside the confines of the military.

With decades of experience under my belt and a wealth of memories to cherish, the prospect of transitioning to civilian life brought a mixture of excitement and uncertainty.

It was during this time that I received unexpected news—I was "selected" to assume control of the Regimental Leadership course in Cyprus. This sudden responsibility arose due to the departure of a Warrant Officer, who had to leave urgently for compassionate reasons. The timing couldn't have been more challenging—the course was due to start in a mere three weeks. Despite the short notice and the weight of this new responsibility, I knew I had to rise to the occasion, mobilising quickly to ensure the smooth execution of the course under these pressing circumstances. With little time to spare, I hastily boarded the next plane bound for the sun-drenched beaches of Cyprus, propelled by a sense of urgency and determination. Drawing on my existing connections and familiarity with the area, I embarked on what many considered a daunting task. Despite the challenges that lay ahead, I was fuelled by the belief that with perseverance and resourcefulness, anything was possible. As the plane soared towards its destination, I braced myself for the whirlwind of activity that awaited.

Twenty days later after a lot of "Begging, Borrowing and Stealing, (Literally), a Lieutenant, a SSgt PTI a drill Sergeant, four Bombardiers AND myself, "welcomed" 35

Gunners at a makeshift old air force camp (with an active airfield) in the Sovereign Base Area (SBA) of Dhekelia.

Over the next four weeks, the Gunners would be pushed to their physical and mental limits through a rigorous training program and an intensive schedule of military subjects focused on honing their leadership skills. Each day brought a fresh set of challenges, ranging from rigorous physical exercises crafted to enhance strength and endurance, to deep-dive discussions and hands-on practical exercises.

We delved into the intricacies of leadership under pressure, combining classroom hard graft with real-world scenarios to hone their abilities. It was an approach I only knew too well, aimed at fostering resilience, adaptability, and the ability to lead effectively in any situation. As running this course brought back memories as I too attended such a course over 21 years ago.

As each challenge was met with determination and resolve, our students grew not only in skill but also in character, ready to face whatever obstacles lay ahead on their leadership journey.

Throughout the program, emphasis would be placed not only on individual performance but also on teamwork through shared challenges and collaborative tasks they would learn to trust and rely on each other.
As they navigated through the demanding curriculum, they would emerge not only as stronger and more capable leaders but also have the qualification to be promoted to a Junior Non-Commissioned Officer (JNCO).

PART II:
New beginnings

Chapter 15

TESOL

As my tenure in the Army approached its conclusion, I found myself at a crossroads, (I have lost count of the number of crossroads I have encountered!!!) contemplating my next career move.

With my ability in German not meeting the requirements for managerial positions, I embarked on a journey to transition into a field where language proficiency was paramount: teaching English. Recognising the demand for English educators in Germany and beyond, I made the decision to pursue a career as an English teacher, a path that led me to undertake the Teaching English to Speakers of Other Languages (TESOL) course paid for by the Army.

Opting for the TESOL course was a strategic choice, driven by the understanding that fluency in English is highly sought after globally. This certification would equip me with the necessary skills to teach English effectively to non-native speakers, opening doors to opportunities not only in Germany but also around the world. However, the path to obtaining this qualification was anything but easy.

The TESOL course proved to be an arduous undertaking, demanding a significant investment of time, effort, and dedication. As I delved into the intricacies of language teaching methodologies, lesson planning, and linguistic theory, I found myself immersed in a world that challenged me intellectually and pushed me beyond my comfort zone. Late nights and early mornings became the norm as I poured over course materials, completed assignments, and prepared for assessments.

There was one particularly gruelling occasion when I found myself working tirelessly through the night, driven by the determination to excel in the course. Despite the fatigue and the daunting nature of the task at hand, I stayed steadfast in my commitment to achieving excellence. Every lesson plan crafted, every grammar rule mastered, and every teaching technique honed brought me one step closer to my goal.

The perseverance and diligence paid off when I received the news that I had passed the TESOL course with distinction. The sense of accomplishment was profound, confirming the countless hours invested in honing my skills as an English educator. Armed with my TESOL certification, I was now equipped to embark on a new chapter in my career journey, ready to make a meaningful impact as an English teacher.

Chapter 16

From Military Service to Home Renovation.

A DIY Tiling Journey

As my military contract drew to a close, my wife and I made the bold decision to embark on a home renovation project. With some savings set aside and a love for do-it-yourself (DIY) projects, we envisioned transforming our home into a space that reflected our style and personality. Little did we know that our decision to renovate would lead us down an unexpected path, one filled with challenges, determination and ultimately, triumph.

Our renovation plans centred around three key areas of our home: the bathrooms, lounge and kitchen. Inspired by the timeless elegance of rough stone Italian marble, we set our sights on incorporating this luxurious material into our design scheme. However, as we began to explore the cost of hiring professionals to execute our vision, well let's just say It was like being kicked between the legs!

During a consultation with a tiling company, we were given a quote that nearly knocked the wind out of us. Eighteen thousand euros for the labour alone, with an additional twelve thousand euros for the cost of the tiles. It was a daunting figure, one that seemed out of reach for our budget. Despite the initial setback, we refused to let discouragement dampen our enthusiasm for the project.

Determined to take matters into our own hands, I made the decision to tackle the tiling myself, much to the disbelief of my wife. With a background in the military, I was no stranger to hard work and perseverance. Yet, I knew that tiling required a unique set of skills and expertise.

Undeterred, I seized the opportunity to enrol in a three-week tiling crash course in the UK, funded by the Army and including accommodation.

The tiling course proved to be both mentally and physically demanding, providing me with invaluable knowledge and hands-on experience. From mastering tile cutting techniques to understanding the intricacies of tile placement and grouting, I immersed myself in every aspect of the craft. What initially seemed like a straightforward task revealed itself to be a complex art form, requiring precision, patience and attention to detail.

Upon completing the course, I returned to Germany armed with newfound confidence and a qualification as a certified tiler. Yet, as I drove back home, the enormity of the task that lay ahead weighed heavily on my mind. Tiling our own house was no small feat, and the prospect of bringing our renovation vision to life felt both exhilarating and daunting.

It's surreal to think that it wasn't long after completing my tiling course that my 24 years of service came to an end. Those years were undoubtedly some of the most fulfilling and memorable times of my life.

The final send-off, marked by a ladies' dinner night, served as a poignant farewell and a testament to the bonds formed over decades of service. Being picked up in a Mercedes limousine, my wife and I were treated to an evening of luxury and celebration, surrounded by friends who had become like family. As we were wined and dined into the early hours of the night, I couldn't help but feel a profound sense of gratitude for the experiences shared and the friendships forged during my time in the army.

With the conclusion of my military service, I found myself transitioning swiftly into a new chapter of my life. There was little time to dwell on my departure from the army after such a lengthy tenure, as I immediately immersed myself in the renovation project awaiting me.

With determination and perseverance as my guiding forces, I dove headfirst into my renovation project, approaching each tile with care and precision. What began as a daunting endeavour soon turned into a labour of love, as I saw our home undergo a stunning transformation, one tile at a time. From meticulously laying out patterns to grouting with precision, every step of the process was a testament to our unwavering commitment to turning our renovation dreams into reality.

In conclusion, our journey from military service to DIY home renovation has been one filled with challenges, triumphs and countless lessons learned along the way. Through perseverance, determination and a willingness to learn, we were able to overcome obstacles and achieve our goal of transforming our house into a place we are proud to call home.

Following the completion of tiling my own home, I found myself inundated with requests from German friends seeking my ability to enhance their spaces. Whether it was revamping a kitchen or refurbishing a toilet, the appeal of "mates' rates" seemed to beckon them my way. While initially flattered by their confidence in my abilities, I soon realised that my newfound skill had inadvertently turned me into a sought-after craftsman within my social circle.

As the demands of being the go-to tiler among my German friends grew, I reached a pivotal moment where I had to set boundaries and prioritise my own well-being. Despite the satisfaction of helping friends and the sense of accomplishment in applying my skills, the toll on my physical health became increasingly clear. After 24 years of service in the army, my knees were bearing the brunt of the labour-intensive work involved in tiling. Recognising the importance of self-care and acknowledging the limitations of my body, I made the difficult decision to say, "enough is enough". My tiling days were over.

Carport

My passion for working with wood runs deep, and it appears to be a trait passed down to my eldest son, who initially honed his skills through a rigorous three-year carpentry course.

Despite his ability in carpentry, he chose to chart a different path and has since qualified as a Civil Engineer. While his journey may have diverged from the traditional woodworking route, his background in carpentry has undoubtedly influenced his approach to engineering, instilling in him a practical understanding of materials and construction techniques.

Together, with the invaluable assistance of my two boys, we embarked on ambitious projects to enhance our home. The collaborative effort resulted in the construction of a spacious 6x6 metre carport, providing shelter for our vehicles and adding a practical yet aesthetically pleasing feature to our property.

Building upon this success, we then set our sights on crafting a 5x6 metre veranda, further expanding our outdoor living space and creating a cosy retreat to enjoy moments of relaxation with family and friends.

Chapter 17

English Teacher

Teaching in the Corporate World

Transitioning from completing my TESOL course to stepping into the classroom marked the beginning of an exhilarating yet challenging chapter in my career journey. Securing a position with a prominent language company thrust me into the dynamic world of teaching, where I found myself catering to a diverse array of students, including academics, doctors and professors.

As a lad from Liverpool teaching "Liverpool English," my experience teaching English to a diverse range of students revealed a common desire among them—they sought not just to learn "school" English, but authentic, spoken English.

It became clear an English English teacher could only teach this, someone intimately familiar with the intricacies of colloquialisms, accents and cultural differences inherent to the language.

I recognised the value of bringing a genuine, native English perspective to the classroom, thereby bridging the gap between textbook English and the language as it is spoken in everyday life. By embracing the role of an English English teacher, I was able to create a learning environment where students felt not only engaged but also empowered to communicate confidently in real-world situations.

While the experience was undeniably rewarding, it was not without its share of stressors, particularly navigating the expectations and demands of teaching high-profile clients.

My journey as an English educator took me to some of the world's largest corporations, including renowned companies like Miele and Bertelsmann. In these corporate settings, my role extended beyond mere language instruction; it encompassed facilitating communication and fostering comprehension in specialised fields ranging from household appliances to sophisticated machinery. Whether explaining the intricacies of a vacuum cleaner to the operation of a multi-million-pound milling machine, I found myself tasked with bridging the gap between technical jargon and everyday English.

Despite the inherent challenges, I approached each lesson with dedication and creativity, tailoring my teaching methods to suit the specific needs and interests of my students.

I also integrated some of my own personal stories and life experiences to provide context and engagement—a strategy that resonated with my students and fostered a deeper connection within the classroom.

Reflecting on my time spent teaching in the corporate arena, I can confidently say that the journey has been immensely gratifying. While the pressure of catering to high-profile clients and delivering specialised content posed its share of challenges, the opportunity to make a meaningful impact through language education made every moment worthwhile.

It is a surreal sensation to realise that in the confines of global business, where English is the preferred language, I have played a pivotal role in facilitating these meetings.

Knowing my former students seamlessly engage in international transactions, negotiations and collaborations with ease and confidence is truly gratifying. Knowing that I have contributed to their ability to navigate the complexities of business communication in English fills me with a profound sense of pride and accomplishment. In a world where effective communication is paramount, the impact of language education cannot be overstated.

Teaching Through Humour

As an English teacher, my classroom was not just a space for learning; it was a stage for storytelling. Nicknamed "The Storyteller" by some of my students, I embraced this title as a testament to my teaching philosophy - a blend of education and entertainment that left a lasting impression on those I taught. One such story is one I told a class of eight women all with a degree in, "something".

With a mischievous twinkle in my eye, I embarked on a story that blurred the lines between reality and, "crossing the line."

"I am really sorry I am late. As I was driving through the German countryside, "Because I got High by Afroman", came on, "WDR 4 radio" the warm summer air blowing on my skin, carrying with it the scent of blooming flowers and freshly cut grass, holding my brandy and coke in one hand - just a single, well, perhaps a large single and in my other hand I had just lit a well-deserved cigarette - can't get any better than this."

Continuing my yarn, I amused them with the absurdity of spilling my beverage over my crotch area, a mishap compounded by the ringing of my mobile phone and dropping my Marlboro cigarette between my legs. Their expressions rocked between, "did this really happen" and "he's joking, right?"

I continued with my story. "So, there I was, forced to seek refuge in a service station, desperately drying my trousers with one of those hot air hand dryers." Laughter filled the room, intermingled with the murmurs of disbelief as my students grappled with the absurdity of the tale and once again, "he's joking, right?"

Yet, amidst the laughter, a moment of seriousness appeared. I then confessed, "It was only my second brandy that morning – well, perhaps my third."

Playfully acknowledging the presence of a doctor among us, with a playful smirk, I directed my next question to the doctor, "I am so lucky, if I have a heart attack, (if I only knew then what I know now) you can save me, right?" However, the conversation took an unexpected turn as the student clarified her academic credentials as a Doctor of Science, rather than a medical doctor.

I jestingly teased, “so you’re not a real Doctor?” a momentary hush fell over the room, met with a piercing look that seemed straight out of a comedy skit. In response, the student firmly asserted, “I AM a real Doctor.” Undeterred, I couldn’t resist a playful reply, “Yes, but not a reeeeal Doctor.” The playful exchange left us all in fits of laughter, our classroom filled with the joyous sound of shared amusement.

Adapting to Teaching Challenges during: The COVID Era

Before the onset of the Coronavirus Disease 2019 (COVID-19) pandemic, my life revolved around face-to-face teaching, a fulfilling avenue for interacting with students and building strong working relationships over time. However, when the pandemic struck and ushered in a new era of lockdowns and restrictions, everything changed dramatically. While my wife, a key worker, continued with her duties under strict regulations, I had to pivot swiftly and completely alter my teaching methods.

Gone were the days of in-person interactions; instead, I found myself navigating the world of online teaching platforms like Skype and Teams - a transition I loathed.

As someone who thrived on physical interaction, the shift to virtual classrooms was a challenging adjustment.

Despite my personal dislike to online teaching, the convenience and cost-effectiveness of virtual platforms made them the preferred choice for many of the companies I taught. With students scattered across different cities like Berlin and Munich, remote teaching became the new norm, further solidifying the dominance of digital learning.

However, the transition came with its own set of challenges, from technical glitches and internet connectivity issues to the lack of genuine human interaction. Nevertheless, I persevered, keeping a disciplined routine of preparation and delivery.

Every Sunday, I dedicated hours to meticulously planning lesson content for the week ahead, ensuring that each student received personalised attention and comprehensive instruction. Yet, as the demands of teaching multiplied with multiple companies and dozens of students, the stress began to take its toll on me. Sundays, once a day of rest and relaxation, became synonymous with anxiety and dread as the pressure to prepare lesson plans loomed over me.

Despite the challenges posed by the COVID epidemic and its aftermath, I soldiered on, driven by a commitment to supporting my students through unprecedented times, even as the weight of virtual teaching bore down heavily on my shoulders.

PART III:
Things start going, "Pete Tong"

Sequence of Events

January 2021
Started having heart pain

16 February 2021
Coronary angiogram - first stent

November 2022
Doctor informed me I will need to start Hormone Replacement Treatment - (Low Testosterone)

November 2022
My dentist said I need to see a specialist to have a tooth removed because of my toothache

7 December 2022
Heart attack - second stent

15 December 2022
Discharged from hospital

17 December 2022
HRT cancelled due to heart attack

January 2023
I informed my doctor that I was experiencing heart pain

6 January 2023
Rushed into A&E - Diverticular disease (again) Stayed in hospital for 5 days

31 January 2023
Coronary angiogram - Third stent

24 Feb - 24 Mar 2023
Heart REHAB - Gollwitzer-Meier-Klinik - Live in patient (4 weeks)

2 April 2023
Heart Pain - Coronary angiogram

8 May 2023
Hypnotherapist

10 May 2023
Tooth out - Minden hospital

30 May 2023
Psychiatrist - Started taking LORAZEPAM/ TAVOR

1 June 2023
Started taking Sertraline

3 June 2023
Rushed into A&E - Diverticular disease (again). Refused to be admitted - they would not operate due to me taking blood thinners

14 June 2023
My Psychologist told me that LORAZEPAM/ TAVOR was the Devil Drug

16 June 2023
Stopped taking LORAZEPAM/ TAVOR

22 June 2023
Breakdown - admitted myself into a mental health hospital - Given maximum dose of LORAZEPAM/TAVOR

9 August 2023
Discharged from mental health hospital

9 August 2024
One year on
I'm still here, still moving forward, still learning how to navigate those bloody waves.

Chapter 18

Heart Pain

In the chill of January 2021, a sense of unease settled upon me as I first encountered chest discomfort.

Ignoring the warning signs of burning, tightness and radiating pain in my neck, jaw and shoulders, I brushed off the symptoms as mere heartburn.

As the days unfolded, the symptoms persisted and intensified, casting a shadow of doubt over my well-being.

Even the simplest tasks, like gardening, became arduous endeavours as I battled against the relentless grip of pain and breathlessness. Despite my attempts to downplay their significance, the symptoms refused to be ignored, growing stronger and lasting longer with each passing day.

Faced with the undeniable reality of my deteriorating health, I sought solace in the ability of my GP (General Practitioner), who wasted no time in referring me to a heart specialist. Submerged in a whirlwind of medical evaluations, I found myself subjected to an array of tests whose purpose eluded me, their significance shrouded in mystery.

Amidst the haze of uncertainty, a pivotal moment during an indoor bicycle exercise test brought clarity to my specialist's diagnosis. With a piercing stab of pain in my heart, the gravity of my condition was laid bare, prompting a decisive course of action.

Recognising the urgency of my situation, my specialist wasted no time in recommending a coronary angiogram, a procedure designed to unveil the mysteries of my ailing heart.

As the fateful day dawned, I embarked on a journey into the unknown, my heart heavy with trepidation as I stepped into the sterile confines of the hospital's operating room. Stripped of my dignity, I prepared myself for the invasive procedure that lay ahead.

Entering the operating theatre, I was greeted by a surreal array of modern medical marvels, the sterile surroundings a stark contrast to the chaos raging within me. Awake throughout the procedure, I watched in awe as the medical team worked with precision and efficiency, navigating the intricate process with practiced ease.

With a small incision made in my groin, I braced myself for the inevitable discomfort, steeling my nerves as the medical team started the angiogram. Despite the invasive nature of the procedure, I felt only a fleeting prick of pain as the specialists worked to insert the necessary equipment.

In a matter of minutes, my fate hung in the balance as the specialists implanted a stent, a beacon of hope in the midst of uncertainty. For me, the journey was far from over, but with each beat of my newly fortified heart, I embraced the promise of a brighter tomorrow.

As I settled into the rhythm of recovery, I found myself reflecting on the surreal nature of my experience, grappling with the profound implications of my brush with mortality. Yet, amidst the uncertainty, there lingered a sense of gratitude for the swift intervention that had potentially saved my life.

As I lay in the hospital bed, recovering from the procedure, I found myself reflecting on the choices that had led me to this moment. The "laissez-faire" attitude with which I had approached my health suddenly seemed reckless and irresponsible.

Reflecting on the following 4 paragraphs fills me with a profound sense of regret and shame.

Despite the warnings and the signs, I had continued to indulge in habits that put my life at risk. Smoking and drinking. I had ignored the consequences, believing myself to be invincible.

With great regret, the significance of what had happened had not sunk in fully, and I continued to live as if nothing had changed. Little did I know that my ignorance would come back to haunt me with a vengeance.

Ten months later, the consequences of my actions came crashing down upon me with brutal force. The warning signs that I had ignored manifested themselves in a devastating heart attack, a cruel reminder of the price of my complacency.

Looking back, I am filled with a sense of disbelief at my own attitude after the first operation. How could I have been so blind to the reality of my situation? How could I have continued to live as if I were invincible, ignoring the warnings and the signs that were so clearly pointing towards disaster?

The answer, of course, lies in the complexity of human nature – in our tendency to deny the reality of our mortality until it is thrust upon us in the most painful and undeniable of ways. I may not be able to undo the mistakes of the past, but I can learn from them and strive to live a life that is worthy of the second chance that has been given to me.

Chapter 19

Heart Attack

The pages I've been dreading to write, the chapters I've been postponing, are finally upon me. It's the part of my story that replays in my mind like a haunting melody - my heart attack. But to utterly understand the weight of that moment, we must rewind the tape and trace the steps leading up to it.

After my first stent insertion, I foolishly continued living life as if nothing had changed. The summer of 2022 passed by like any other, but subtle signs were beginning to surface. I found myself gasping for breath more often, putting it down to the inevitable toll of aging – after all, as the saying goes, "I'm not getting any younger."

In early October, I started having a bad toothache that just wouldn't go away and to make matters worse, I also had a nagging earache. When I went to see the dentist about it, they said I needed to have the tooth removed, which made me feel really anxious. But then, they dropped another bombshell - they couldn't do the extraction themselves, so I'd have to go to a different dentist who specialises in tooth extraction. I've always been terrified of going to the dentist, so just the thought of having this procedure done sent shivers down my spine.

I really want to stress how terrified I am of dentists, the needles and drilling especially when they need to pull out a tooth. It's like just the thought of it makes me feel so uneasy. I've spent a lot of time in war zones, and one of the things that scared me the most was the idea of being captured and tortured using methods like tooth extraction.

The idea of going through that kind of pain and discomfort is just too much for me to handle. It's like a nightmare I never want to experience.

During that month, I also felt like something was off, but I couldn't quite figure out what it was. I was always tired, easily irritated, and lacked my usual enthusiasm. It felt like I had lost my motivation and energy. I even wondered if I was going through a midlife crisis. To get some answers, I went to see my doctor, and he did a blood test. The results revealed a low testosterone count, prompting a referral to an endocrinologist for further investigation.

After scheduling my appointment, I had to undergo another blood test. As I've mentioned before, I'm afraid of dentists, and I also fear needles!

After getting a call from the doctor, I found out my testosterone levels were really low, which I already knew from my GP. He suggested I try Hormone Replacement Therapy, something I hadn't heard about until then. The medical term for this condition is Hypogonadism, but it's also referred to as "Male Menopause". This was all new information to me, and I had a lot to learn about what it meant for my health.

To talk about what I could do next, my "hormone doctor" set up a meeting for me in early December to go over "my options".

All these visits to the doctor and discussions about my health were really starting to overwhelm me and make me feel anxious. Trying to keep up with all the medical terms and treatments they talked about during my appointments was really challenging. On top of that, there was also the language barrier to deal with, which made everything even more confusing and difficult to understand. It felt like I was swimming in a sea of unfamiliar words and concepts, desperately struggling for breath.

Each appointment added to my mounting anxiety, compounded by my fear of needles and the overwhelming complexity of medical jargon. Meanwhile, symptoms reminiscent of my first cardiac episode began to resurface, this time with heightened intensity and frequency.

One Wednesday morning (7 December 2022 to be precise), around three o'clock, I woke up feeling a sharp pain in my chest. Desperate for relief, I got up and ran on the spot for a few minutes, which helped ease the pain temporarily. When I climbed back into bed, I realised I should see my doctor that morning. After my wife left for work, I got up, showered and shaved, but once again, I felt stabbing pain in my chest. Despite this, I got dressed in smart attire and began the short walk to my GP's office.

As I entered the front door of the surgery, I suddenly felt my mouth go dry, and I became dizzy and off balance. The nurses at once noticed and rushed to help me, guiding me into a treatment room. My doctor arrived and quickly identified the situation – I was having a heart attack.

Memories of, "Drifting Off."

As I reflect on this section of the book, I realise it holds deeper meaning for me beyond just words on a page. It seems to be a catalyst for my mental breakdown, stirring up emotions and thoughts that are difficult to handle.

I remember lying on the floor surrounded by my doctor and three nurses, I heard the screaming siren sounds of ambulances screaming to a halt outside the surgery.

The side doors opened, and a quick response doctor followed by 4 paramedics burst into the surgery. I was clutching at my GP's leg, shouting at him to tell my wife and kids, "I'm sorry and I love them." I said this at least ten times then I started screaming the same words but telling my GP to actually go to my house and tell her.

I then noticed a paramedic towering over me with what seemed like a 30-inch needle. At this moment I felt myself, "drifting away" briefly regaining consciousness in the ambulance I once again, "drifted off" but this time my heart stopped.

Awakening in a sterile white room, I am flooded with relief and disbelief at my continued existence. The vivid recollection of the moments preceding my lapse into unconsciousness spurs a torrent of emotions, manifesting in tearful exclamations of gratitude for my survival. My urgent pleas to reach out to my loved one's echoed through the room, a testament to the depth of my love and the gravity of the situation.

I was told to, "be quiet," as another patient was undergoing a similar ordeal to me in the next room. Transferred to the cardiac ward, I was subjected to relentless monitoring, a constant reminder of the fragility of life and the urgency of my recovery.

My ordeal unfolds against the backdrop of the COVID era, with strict visiting regulations adding another layer of complexity to an already difficult journey. The agonising wait to reunite with my wife and children serves as a poignant reminder of the importance of human connection in times of crisis.

When the long-awaited reunion finally arrived, the restrictions allowing only one visitor at a time failed to contain the floodgates of emotion that burst open. Despite the overwhelming relief of being reunited with my loved ones, a sense of urgency gnawed at me, reminding me of the things left unsaid and the love left unexpressed. Amidst tears and embraces, my paramount concern was conveying the depth of my love and gratitude to my wife and my two boys.

In the days that followed, I was subjected to tests and more tests, each yielding positive results and offering reassurance of my improving condition. Discharged from the hospital with strict instructions to mend my lifestyle habits, stop smoking and drinking. I embark on a journey of recovery with newfound determination and resolve.

When I talked to my endocrinologist, who specialises in hormone-related issues, about starting Hormone Replacement Treatment (HRT), he at once said we couldn't do it. This was because of my heart attack and the medications I was already taking. It was a tough decision, but he thought it was best for my health and safety.

I am confronted with the sobering reality of the impact of my health on my overall well-being. The revelation that low testosterone levels may contribute to stress, depression and anxiety serves as a sobering reminder of the interconnectedness of physical and mental health.

Retirement

While lying in bed a few days after my heart attack, I made a major decision – I would retire from teaching. This choice weighed heavily on my heart, as I had developed strong relationships with my students and colleagues.

My boss refused to accept my retirement, insisting that I could take as much time off as I needed, whether it be six months or a year, with the hope that I would eventually return. I agreed, holding onto the possibility of returning to teaching once my health improved.

Little did I know at the time that my health would take another significant blow. Although I wouldn't miss spending Sunday afternoons preparing lesson plans, I knew I would miss the small talk with my students dearly.

Defibrillation and Severe Depression, Anxiety and PTSD

One day, out of the blue, I asked my wife, “Hey babe, I wonder if having my heart started using a defibrillator has anything to do with my mental illness.”

After spending countless hours researching, I realised I’m not the only one pondering this question.

Despite all the information I found, I still believe there’s more research needed to fully understand this connection. While I’ve come across some insights, I’m aware that I’m not equipped to answer all the technical questions.

So, here are my findings:

While there isn’t a definitive answer yet, there seems to be a link between defibrillator use and mental health.

Many people who’ve had similar experiences have wondered about this connection, suggesting that it’s a topic worth exploring further.

Ultimately, I’ll leave the in-depth analysis to the professionals. But for now, it’s clear there’s a need for more research to shed light on the relationship between defibrillator use and mental illness.

The relationship between having your heart restarted using a defibrillator and clinical depression, anxiety and PTSD can be quite complex.

While the physical experience of undergoing a defibrillation procedure may not directly cause depression or anxiety, the emotional and psychological impact of such an event can significantly affect a person's mental health.

Firstly, the experience of having a defibrillator used on you can be traumatic and frightening.

It often occurs during life-threatening situations, such as sudden cardiac arrest, which can be a terrifying ordeal. The fear and uncertainty surrounding such an event can leave a lasting emotional impact on individuals, potentially triggering symptoms of anxiety or post-traumatic stress disorder (PTSD).

Individuals who undergo defibrillation procedures may face ongoing concerns about their health and mortality. They may worry about the underlying heart condition that led to the need for defibrillation and the risk of future cardiac events.

These worries can contribute to feelings of anxiety and hypertension vigilance, as individuals become hyper-aware of any changes or sensations in their bodies.

In addition to these emotional challenges, individuals who have experienced cardiac events or have underlying heart conditions may be at a higher risk of developing depression.

Chronic illnesses and life-threatening experiences can disrupt one's sense of normalcy and lead to feelings of sadness, hopelessness and despair.

While there may not be a direct relationship between defibrillation and severe depression, anxiety and PTSD, the emotional and psychological impact of undergoing such procedures and living with heart-related concerns can significantly influence a person's mental health.

It's essential for individuals who have undergone defibrillation or have heart conditions to prioritise their emotional well-being and seek support from healthcare professionals, counsellors, or support groups if needed.

Chapter 20

Follow up medical problems

Experiencing a heart attack followed by ongoing health complications can be an incredibly challenging journey, both physically and emotionally.

In early January 2023, amidst dealing with constant toothache and recurring chest pains reminiscent of my earlier heart attack, I found myself once again in distress.

This time, the pains in my groin Indicated the return of Diverticular disease, a condition I had battled before.

Rushed to the hospital and admitted to the Intensive Care Unit (ICU), I began a treatment plan of pain relief and intravenous antibiotics, all while navigating the added stress of the ongoing COVID-19 pandemic.

Days in the ICU felt like an eternity, as I grappled with multiple health issues and the discomfort of countless needles, a fear I've long harboured. Despite medical attention and the support of loved ones, including limited visitation due to pandemic restrictions, the pain persisted.

While in the hospital receiving medical attention for my Diverticular disease and dealing with chest pain, toothache and earache, my doctor connected the earache to the toothache and suggested that the chest pains might be side effects of my heart medication. Fortunately, the pain from all three issues was lessened by the strong painkillers I received for my colon pain. The prospect of surgery for Diverticular disease loomed, but was postponed due to my recent heart attack, adding to the weight of uncertainty and anxiety.

Attempting to quit smoking amidst these health challenges proved daunting, highlighting the complexities of addiction and stress management. Despite efforts to break free from the habit, the grip of addiction remained strong, worsening an already tumultuous situation.

Eventually released from the hospital, my toothache persisted, prompting a nerve-wracking visit to an emergency dental specialist in Bielefeld. With the support of my youngest son, navigating logistical challenges and language barriers, I hoped for relief from the constant pain.

However, my hopes were dashed when the dentist, upon learning of my recent heart attack and extensive medication programme, declined to go ahead with the procedure. Instead, I was directed to seek treatment from a specialised dentist at a hospital in Minden.

Coronary angiogram - Third stent

Realising that my chest pain felt like when I had my heart attack, my heart doctor ran all the usual tests, but everything seemed normal. Despite this, he decided to do a coronary angiogram just to be safe. My wife took the day off to go with me to the hospital for the procedure, but she was told she would receive a call when I was ready to be discharged.

Alone in the operating room once again, I felt nervous knowing I would be awake for the entire procedure. It felt like déjà vu. I woke up later in the afternoon in a recovery room with my wife by my side, listening to one of her audiobooks. The doctor came in and explained that he found a narrowed artery and had to implant another stent.

This experience prompted me to make some significant life changes, including quitting smoking and attending the Heart Rehabilitation Centre in Bad Oeynhausen, which I had previously put off because it meant being away from home for four weeks.

Chapter 21

Heart REHAB: Gollwitzer-Meier-Klinik

On February 24th, 2023, I made a momentous decision to admit myself to the Gollwitzer-Meier-Klinik in Bad Oeynhausen.

Situated on the southern edge of Minden, Bad Oeynhausen is known as a spa town and is nationally recognised as a health centre for regeneration and healing.

For me, this day marked not only the beginning of my journey towards healing but also the moment I made a life-changing decision to quit smoking.

As soon as I stepped over the threshold of the clinic, I put an end to my smoking addiction, and to this day, I haven't touched another cigarette. However, despite my commitment to quitting, I still miss smoking greatly.

Entering the Gollwitzer-Meier-Klinik, I was struck by the sense of efficiency, almost like a conveyor belt, with COVID protocols still very much in place. The atmosphere felt overly militarised, with instructions to go here, go there, and report back once tasks were completed.

The language barrier was once again a significant challenge, as the lady at reception spoke no English. After being handed countless forms to sign, I was finally shown to my room, which was surprisingly spacious and had a large balcony.

However, the bureaucratic process took up most of the morning, and by the time it was over, it was already lunchtime.

Due to COVID restrictions, meal timings were staggered, and I found myself allocated to the second serving. Instead of the usual buffet service, tables were assigned to individuals for table service. It felt strange to eat alone at my own table, but the food was satisfactory, albeit lacking in quantity and seasoning.

I was informed that I would receive a weekly program by the end of the day, but before that, I had an appointment with my allocated heart doctor in the afternoon.

However, the doctor's appointment didn't go as smoothly as expected. He began speaking rapidly in German, leaving me feeling overwhelmed and stressed. It wasn't until he realised, I was English that he switched to Russian, I know, Russian. Then, unexpectedly, he asked if I spoke Russian, which caught me off guard and added to my frustration.

Feeling frustrated and disheartened, I expressed my regrets and said that being there was a mistake before leaving the office and heading for the door, feeling an immediate dislike for the place. Thankfully, a nurse who spoke English followed me, reassuring me that they were actively searching for an English-speaking doctor and providing some comfort in the midst of my frustration.

Eventually, I was assigned a doctor who spoke English decently enough. Looking back, this marked the beginning of my journey with mental illness. As I sat down in his office, I found myself unable to stop crying, overwhelmed by emotions with no clear understanding of the cause, which only added to my stress. After what felt like an eternity, we concluded our appointment.

Concerned by my emotional state, the doctor arranged for an emergency appointment with a psychologist later that afternoon.

This sudden turn of events sent conflicting messages racing through my mind. I couldn't help but question why I needed to see a psychologist. After all, I was there to address my heart issues, not my mental health. The idea of seeing a "shrink" made me feel confused and defensive, as I grappled with the stigma surrounding mental health and the perceived implications of needing psychological support.

On a late Friday afternoon, I had my appointment with the psychologist who had been assigned to me. He spoke perfect English and had a calming tone. As soon as I sat down, I burst into uncontrollable sobs. This reaction terrified me, and I struggled to comprehend why I was feeling this way. After I explained about my heart attack, the psychologist reassured me that my reactions were completely normal, but I still found it difficult to process all these new emotions. The hour-long appointment flew by, leaving me feeling disoriented and unsure if I was coming or going, all on my very first day.

During the four weeks I spent in the Heart Rehabilitation Centre, my schedule wasn't packed, but I made sure to engage in physical activities every day and my wife and kids visited me every weekend, which brought me comfort and support. Additionally, I had four more sessions with my psychologist during this time.

During the four weeks I was experiencing moments of great sadness and despair. Having no idea what was going on I kept on telling myself to, "man up, get a grip."

My psychologist strongly encouraged me to keep up with weekly therapy sessions and even provided me with the contact information for a reputable English-speaking psychologist in my area. At the time, I had no idea why he emphasised this so strongly, but little did I know, he sensed the storm of mental illness looming on the horizon, something entirely unfamiliar to me that was about to change my life in unimaginable ways.

Dental consultation

During my time at the heart REHAB centre, I had a dental consultation in Minden, and my eldest son accompanied me to help with the language barrier, which was causing me more stress than usual.

The hospital where the consultation took place was massive, which for some reason made me feel uneasy. However, the dentist I saw spoke American English and was incredibly reassuring.

Despite my fear, she made me feel comfortable and assured me that everything would be okay.

Since my pain wasn't severe enough to be considered an emergency, the earliest available date for the tooth extraction was May 10, 2023, six weeks away. Initially, I felt relieved to have some time to prepare mentally, but looking back, I realised I should have pushed for an earlier appointment. Additionally, the dentist informed me that I would need to stay in the hospital after the procedure due to my heart medication.

Coronary angiogram

On March 28, 2023, I visited my heart doctor once again, complaining of, you guessed it, chest pain. Without conducting any tests, he immediately scheduled me for another Coronary angiogram.

The day of the procedure arrived on April 2nd, and it felt like déjà vu, again. I knew exactly what to expect, but whether this was a good or bad thing, I couldn't say for sure.

During the angiogram, everything went smoothly, but surprisingly, no stent was needed this time. Instead, my doctor shared some puzzling news with me. He explained that there was an artery in my heart that was almost closed, but even if it closed completely, it wouldn't have any impact, as if it had no function. He suggested that this might be contributing to my ongoing chest pains. It was a lot of information to absorb and process.

In response to the news about my artery, I bombarded my doctor with questions. I asked when it would close, if I would feel it when it does, what would happen when it closes, if my chest pain would go away, and how to differentiate between chest pains and a heart attack.

Unfortunately, his answer to all my questions was the same: he didn't know for sure. Even now, I'm unsure whether the artery has closed or not, as I continue to experience daily chest pains.

Hypnotherapist

As I recovered from my Coronary angiogram, the lingering groin pain and the impending tooth extraction weighed heavily on my mind with each passing day.

Feeling increasingly anxious, a friend suggested seeing a hypnotherapist, a thought that had never crossed my mind before. In a state of desperation, I was willing to try anything to ease my worries.

After thorough research online, I found a hypnotherapist with glowing reviews, a Scottish practitioner in Bielefeld. Taking a leap of faith, I called him and explained my situation, almost pleading for a consultation. To my relief, he agreed to meet on the 4th of May to discuss the process and cost.

On the appointed day, we had our meeting, and I was in a mindset where I was willing to try any solution offered. We set a date for the hypnotherapy session, which took place just four days later. Despite some nerves, I tried to keep a positive outlook on the experience.

Accompanied by my youngest son, I arrived at the hypnotherapist's clinic and was led to a serene room with a reclining chair at its centre.

Feeling apprehensive but determined, I settled into the chair as the hypnotherapist covered me with blankets and played soft music to create a soothing atmosphere. He began reassuring me that I was not afraid of dentists, and before I knew it, I was waking up from what felt like a deep, comforting sleep.

Upon being prompted to look at the clock, I was surprised to realise that over an hour had passed, though it felt like mere minutes to me.

As I emerged from the session, still processing the experience, I inquired if it had been successful. The hypnotherapist cryptically replied, "time will tell", before excusing himself.

After composing myself, I made the payment of 400 euros and was bid farewell with a wish of good luck.
Feeling somewhat bewildered by the session's effects, I decided to keep an open mind as my hospital appointment loomed just two days away.

Tooth Extraction

The dreaded day finally arrived as I, accompanied by my wife and eldest son, made my way to Minden Hospital for the inevitable tooth extraction. With an overnight bag packed and nerves running high, I checked myself in at reception before settling into my hospital room and unpacking my belongings.

Shortly thereafter, a nurse entered and informed me that the procedure was scheduled for two hours later, recommending that I take the Pre-Med tablet. Little did I know that this seemingly innocuous tablet would become the catalyst for a profound shift in my mental state.

As the tablet took effect, I began to feel strangely relaxed and somewhat "floppy", a stark departure from the anxiety that had consumed me earlier. An hour later, I found myself in a spacious operating theatre, surrounded by three assistants and, to my relief, the same dentist who gave me my consultation. Her constant reassurance provided a sense of comfort as she administered the local anaesthesia, with my wife and son by my side for support.

Surprisingly, I stayed remarkably calm even when informed of a slight complication that would prolong the procedure. Despite the sensation of someone "digging for gold with a high-pitched drill", my mind wandered to serene imagery of enjoying a Cornish pasty while watching waves crash against the Cornish coast.

While sitting in the dental chair, I pondered the source of my newfound composure. Was it the effective functioning of the Pre-Med tablet, or had the hypnotherapy session played a role? Perhaps it was a combination of both.

Twenty minutes later, the procedure concluded, and I expressed my gratitude to the dentist with a heartfelt hug before returning to my room. Despite resembling someone who had been struck across the face with a sock filled with billiard balls, I felt a sense of relief wash over me.

An hour later, the doctor delivered the welcome news that I could return home, as the procedure had gone smoothly, and the bleeding had ceased. Reflecting on the experience, I marvelled at how all the stress and fear had dissipated within the span of a few short hours. A question still lingers, "did the hypnosis actually work" as I found myself returning to the dentist with markedly less trepidation.

Chapter 22

Rob

I included this unplanned chapter in my book because right after finishing chapter 21, my friend contacted me, revealing he's experiencing another breakdown. Yesterday, he sent me a poem.

He's struggling to find the right words to express just how "shit" he's feeling, a challenge that I am all too familiar with. Despite the difficulty, he's turned to writing poetry as a way to capture and communicate his emotions. It serves as a poignant reminder of the immense struggle we face in articulating our feelings, especially during times of overwhelming debilitation.

I've made the decision to dedicate a chapter of my book to discussing what to say, or more importantly, what not to say, when a family member or friend is experiencing these difficult emotions. Knowing how to communicate effectively can make a significant difference in providing comfort and help to those who are struggling.

He stood on the bridge
in silence and fear,
For the demons of darkness
Had driven him here.

They cut his heart
Right out of his chest,
making him believe
That the demons knew best.

They were always there,
sometimes just out of sight,
waiting in the background
till the time was right.

These demons were destructive,
knocking down the life he knew,
hating everything about him;
He hated himself, too.

These demons cannot be seen,
But they're far from fairy tales.
They live inside your mind;
Their evilness prevails.

So, on the bridge he stood,
about to end the fight.
Then he stopped and thought
I'll fight them one more night..........

If you're worried that a family member or friend might be suffering from depression, anxiety, PTSD, or a combination of all three, there are several steps you can take to offer support.

Talking to them about your concerns and what you've seen can be a good starting point. Let them know that you care about them and that you're there to support them.

Encourage them to seek professional help and offer to accompany them to appointments if they're willing. Reassure them that seeking help is not a sign of weakness and that it's okay to ask for support.

There's no quick fix or miracle cure for any Mental illness. Recovery is a process that takes time. By being there for your loved one and offering support, you can make a positive difference in their journey towards healing.

Some comments can do more harm than good. For example, saying "It's all in your head" dismisses the reality of mental illness, which is not imaginary but a genuine struggle.

Comparing their problems to others and saying "things could be worse" can belittle their experiences and invalidate their feelings.

Telling someone to "snap out of it" implies that they have control over their illness, when in reality, there's no simple on/off switch for mental health issues.

Saying things like “You have a great life, why are you feeling shitty?” ignores the complexity of mental illness and implies that external circumstances should determine one’s mental state.

It’s also unhelpful to suggest that their struggles will just pass on their own, as mental health issues often require professional support and treatment.

Comments like, “It’s God’s plan” can feel like their suffering is being reduced to a simple phrase. It can come across as if their deep and complex emotions are not being fully acknowledged. This can make them feel isolated and invalidated, as though their experiences are not being taken seriously.

However, it’s important to recognise that for some, faith and spirituality play a significant role in their coping mechanisms. For them, hearing “It’s God’s plan” can be comforting and provide a sense of reassurance or purpose during tough times.

This is a tricky and complicated subject. Understanding their personal beliefs and what comforts them can help guide your choice of words.

Ultimately, the best approach is to listen to your family member or friend and communicate in a way that respects their feelings and beliefs. Offering empathy and understanding is key to providing meaningful support.

I cannot emphasise enough how crucial it is to prioritise your own well-being while providing support to someone with depression.

Supporting a loved one through depression can take a toll on your emotional health, so it's essential to take care of yourself too.

Below are bullet points intended for quick guidance:

The following 7 phrases are **helpful things** to say:

1. "I'm here for you": Let them know that you're available to listen and support them through this tough time.

2. "It's okay to not be okay": Assure them that it's normal to struggle with mental health challenges and that they're not alone in their experience.

3. "I believe in you": Offer words of encouragement and express confidence in their ability to overcome this challenging period.

4. "You're brave for reaching out": Acknowledge their courage in seeking help or opening up about their struggles.

5. "How can I support you right now?": Show genuine interest in understanding their needs and offer practical help, whether it's accompanying them to appointments, helping with daily tasks, or simply being a supportive presence.

6. “It’s okay to take things one step at a time”: Remind them that healing takes time and that it’s okay to focus on small victories and progress.

7. “You’re not alone”: Reassure them that you’re committed to supporting them through their journey and that there are resources and professionals available to help.

The following 7 points are phrases to **avoid** saying:

1. “Just snap out of it”: This dismisses the seriousness of their experience and implies that they can control their mental health struggles simply by willpower alone.

2. “It’s all in your head”: This minimises their feelings and may make them feel like their struggles are not valid or real.

3. “I know how you feel”: While well-intentioned, it can come across as invalidating their unique experience. Instead, offer empathy and support without assuming you fully understand their situation.

4. “You’re overreacting”: This can make them feel judged or misunderstood, worsening their distress.

5. “You should be grateful for what you have”: While gratitude can be helpful, it’s essential to acknowledge their pain and struggles rather than dismissing them.

6. "Just think positive": While positivity can be beneficial, it's not a quick fix for mental health issues. Encourage them to seek professional help if needed and offer support in finding effective coping strategies.

7. "It's probably just stress": Downplaying their experience by attributing it solely to stress may make them feel unheard or invalidated.

Part IV: Breakdown

Chapter 23

Lorazepam/Tavor

Since experiencing uncontrollable episodes of crying back in February, I noticed a troubling escalation of negative emotions that seemed to intensify as time went on.

By early May 2023, I was overwhelmed by feelings of sadness and a general sense of "shittiness," worsened by persistent alertness and the inability to get a good night's sleep.

The cycle of sleep deprivation only served to worsen my emotional turmoil, leading to tearful outbursts over seemingly trivial matters.

Recognising the severity of my symptoms, I sought help from my GP, who prescribed sleeping tablets and recommended I consult with a psychiatrist.

On the morning of May 30th, my youngest son drove me to the psychiatrist's surgery, as I was in no condition to drive myself. Overwhelmed by emotion, I found myself in tears once again as the psychiatrist provided me with a contact number for a reputable English-speaking psychologist and prescribed me 100, 25 mg of Sertraline, an antidepressant.

In addition to the Sertraline, the doctor also prescribed 50, 2mg tablets of TAVOR, recommending that I take one when I felt, "shitty". He cautioned me about the addictive nature of Tavor and warned against exceeding four tablets a day. Despite the doctor's warning, I hastily obtained the prescribed medications from the chemist and immediately took one Sertraline tablet followed by a Tavor tablet.

Within thirty minutes, I began to feel a sense of relaxation that had eluded me for months, as if I were floating on a cloud of tranquillity the same feeling I experienced when I was having my tooth pulled out.

For someone accustomed to seeking quick-fix solutions, the immediate relief provided by Tavor seemed like a miraculous answer to my problems. However, as I reflect on this experience, I realise the importance of approaching mental health treatment with caution and awareness, understanding that medications like Tavor can be addictive and may not offer a sustainable solution to underlying issues.

While medications like Lorazepam/Tavor can offer temporary relief from symptoms, it's crucial to recognise their potential for addiction and the serious risks they pose to one's health and well-being. Despite warnings about the maximum dosage, I occasionally exceeded the recommended limit, seeking refuge in the calming effects it provided.

Over time, I noticed a concerning shift in my emotional state—I felt numb to the world around me, indifferent to things that once mattered. While this worried me, the temporary relief offered by Tavor seemed to outweigh the negative consequences.

Recognising the need for professional support, I followed my psychiatrist's advice and scheduled an appointment with an English-speaking psychologist.

The potential for life-threatening complications associated with misuse or overuse of medications like Lorazepam/Tavor cannot be overstated. It's essential to heed the warnings provided by healthcare professionals and to use these medications responsibly, under their guidance and supervision.

In hindsight, I wish I had taken the time to research and fully understand the implications of the medications prescribed to me. Little did I realise at the time; I was slowly becoming dependent on Tavor.

I only discovered some of the side effects of Lorazepam/Tavor after 8 weeks of being prescribed the medication. It was alarming to learn that anxiety, depression, hallucinations and an increased risk of suicidal thoughts are potential risks associated with its use. This lack of prior information highlights the importance of thorough communication between healthcare providers and patients when it comes to medication side effects.

A&E - Diverticular disease (again)

On the morning of Saturday, June 3rd, 2023, I woke up to an excruciating pain radiating from my left groin area. Ignoring it was futile as the pain persisted and intensified throughout the day. By early evening, realising I could not bear it any longer, I made the decision to seek urgent medical attention at the Accident and Emergency (A&E) department.

Deep down, I harboured a nagging suspicion: Diverticular disease, a familiar foe, had reared its head once again.

Upon arrival at the hospital, the urgency of the situation was clear, and the medical team wasted no time. Pain relief was administered intravenously, swiftly followed by a battery of blood tests to confirm my fears.

Overwhelmed by intense conflicting feelings emotions, I found myself engulfed in tears and gasping for air. It wasn't just the physical pain that weighed heavily on me; it was also the overwhelming sense of despair and helplessness, a feeling I had come to know all too well as "shitty."

The results of the blood tests, coupled with a thorough health assessment, left no room for doubt: Diverticular disease had made its unwelcome return. The diagnosis only served to compound the mental anguish already gnawing at my already broken mind.

The doctor mentioned that typically, they would opt for surgery after experiencing two or more episodes of diverticular disease. However, considering my recent heart attack and the number of heart-related medications I was on, he considered it unwise to go ahead with surgery at this time.

The doctor recommended a minimum of five days of hospitalisation for intensive treatment, but the mere thought of it sent shivers down my spine. Overwhelmed with emotion, I succumbed to uncontrollable trembling and tears.

Recognising the fragile state of my mental health, the doctor made a compassionate decision to forego admission, fearing it would worsen my already precarious emotional state. Instead, we mutually agreed upon a prescribed medical treatment: a course of intravenous antibiotics to be administered immediately followed by oral medication at home. I was instructed to return the following morning for a progress check, a glimmer of hope in an otherwise bleak situation.

That night brimmed with restlessness as I yearned for even a hint of peace. Once more, I sought solace in the haven of the drug I know all too well - Tavor.

Sleep remained difficult to attain, and anxiety steadily increased. Although the pain briefly lessened the following morning, upon reaching the hospital, I met a different doctor who was aware of the events of the previous night. With compassion, he allowed me to continue my treatment at home.

"Devil's Drug"

Following my psychiatrist's recommendation, I arranged a meeting with the English-speaking psychologist he had suggested. Despite her busy schedule, she kindly agreed to meet with me the following week. (June 14, 2023).

My evenings became a struggle, watching TV would often trigger overwhelming emotions, causing me to burst into tears and struggle to breathe. It felt like I was sinking deeper and deeper into a dark pit, with no way out.

Bedtime became a battleground as I tossed and turned my mind in constant overdrive, only to wake up drenched in sweat after brief moments of sleep. It was a frightening experience. Not understanding the source of my emotions intensified my struggles. I relied on a mix of medications to address various health concerns like heart issues, hypertension and depression. Tavor was among them. It dulled my senses, offering fleeting respite from the persistent grip of sorrow.

The following week is a blur in my memory. I remember my wife going with me to the psychologist's office, where the atmosphere was calm and soothing, but I couldn't shake the feeling of unease as my thoughts raced uncontrollably.

During our conversation, I found myself rambling on about assorted topics, unable to make sense of my own thoughts. Attempting to convey the idea of a perfect life only led to more tears and confusion.

When the discussion turned to my medications, I showed the psychologist my plan, her words hit me like a ton of bricks: "Tavor is the Devil's Drug." It was a wake-up call that prompted a pivotal decision—I chose to stop taking Tavor that very day. Little did I know, this decision would lead me down a path I never imagined.

The next five days are a blur of unbearable emotions and confusion. I reached out to my GP in desperation, only to be faced with the daunting suggestion of being admitted to a mental hospital. The mere thought of being labelled with societal stereotypes associated with mental illness sent shivers down my spine. I vehemently declined the recommendation, determined to handle it on my own.

The next 18 hours of my life are a complete blank, lost in a haze of fear and uncertainty. But when I mustered the courage to reach out to my GP again, overwhelmed with emotion, he didn't waste a moment. He immediately offered an emergency admission request, suggesting he could call an ambulance for monitoring, emphasising the urgency of seeking proper medical care.

Despite his offer, I declined the ambulance, haunted by memories of my heart attack. Instead, I insisted on finding my own way to the hospital. With my wife at work and unaware of the unfolding events, I asked my youngest son to drive me to hospital.

Chapter 24

Mental Health Hospital

Arriving at Gilead 4, the mental health hospital that my GP had sent me, I was greeted by a scene I can only describe as chaotic. In the waiting room, a young woman in her twenties was shouting unintelligible words, punctuated by intermittent screams. The sight of blood splattered on the walls and floor, increasing my anxiety even further.

Within half an hour I was ushered into a consultation room, a compassionate nurse efficiently took my blood and conducted an ECG, the needle's prick surprisingly painless. Soon after, a psychiatrist entered, bombarding me with what felt like a thousand questions. I struggled to make sense of it all, my mind a jumble of thoughts and emotions.

From the moment I stepped into the hospital until the moment I was admitted, my youngest son stood faithfully by my side, bearing witness to scenes that no one should ever have to endure. Most distressing of all was watching his dad, once strong and composed, reduced to a cowering wreck. Sam, I am so sorry.

Upon hearing of my hospitalisation, thanks to my son, my wife wasted no time and drove straight to see me. As always, her calm and reassuring demeanour provided me with a much-needed sense of reassurance. In the presence of the psychiatrist, my wife patiently fielded many questions about the events leading up to me seeking help at Gilead 4.

Initial Treatment Plan:

My next step was a consultation with one of the more senior doctors. Accompanied by my wife and the psychiatrist. The head doctor spoke perfect English and outlined her proposed treatment plan.

What was even more shocking was her recommendation to administer the maximum allowable dose of TAVOR. This news was overwhelming, and it felt like a heavy blow because Tavor had played a significant role in the predicament I was currently facing.

Despite the clear risks associated with Tavor, the doctor was clear and confident in her explanation. She acknowledged the dangers but emphasised that, when used correctly and under strict supervision, Tavor could be lifesaving. Her proposal was to start me on the highest permissible dose. The plan was not to keep me on this high dose indefinitely, but to gradually reduce the dosage over time.

As she spoke, I found myself struggling to grasp the gravity of her words. The reality of the situation hit me hard, and I became emotional, breaking down into tears and having trouble in breathing. The doctor, however, remained calm and reassuring. She shared with us her extensive experience of over twenty years in the field of mental health. Furthermore, she disclosed that she had been responsible for the mental health care of British service men and women during their postings in Germany.

Even though I was initially overwhelmed and confused by the consultation, the doctor's manner had a profound impact on me. Despite the clinical setting and the gravity of the situation, she exuded a warmth and concern reminiscent of a caring grandmother. Her top priority was my well-being, which provided a sense of comfort amidst the chaos of my emotions.

The details of that first consultation remain somewhat hazy in my memory, likely due to the emotional turmoil I was experiencing. However, one thing stands out clearly: I gave my consent to be admitted for treatment and to start on Tavor, trusting in the doctor's experience and the comprehensive plan she had laid out.

It was a moment brimming with intense emotions, yet it was also infused with hope. This hope was strengthened by the unwavering support of my wife, the psychiatrist, and the experienced doctor now overseeing my care. Amidst the turmoil, I felt a glimmer of reassurance, knowing that I was in capable hands.

My First 24 Hours in a Mental Health Hospital

My first 24 hours in a mental health hospital are surprisingly clear in my memory. Saying goodbye to my wife, a wave of calm wrapped around me. I knew I had made the right decision and felt safe in this new setting.

The psychiatrist went with me to the ward where I would spend the next six weeks. Upon arrival, I was greeted by a friendly mental health nurse who spoke perfect English, which was a great relief. Contrary to my expectations, none of the staff wore uniforms, which made the atmosphere feel more welcoming.

The nurse showed me around Ward 7. This ward was used for patients attending a nine-week Cognitive Behavioural Therapy (CBT) course, as well as for patients like me, who were in crisis. Her warm and welcoming demeanour helped ease my anxiety, and I began to feel more relaxed in this unfamiliar place.

After arriving, the nurse arranged a late lunch for me. As I ate, she went over the hospital's "dos and don'ts" and I couldn't help but notice that all the windows had deadbolt locks. The nurse then took me to my shared room. The hospital was full, so they had converted a single room into a double. The room was small, and like the other windows, the window had a deadbolt lock. I was informed that my roommate was on day release and would be back in a few hours.

Despite the whirlwind of emotions racing through my mind, I felt optimistic, thinking, "They are going to fix me, and I'll be out of here in no time." (Nearly a year later, as I write my book, I'm not 100% fixed).

The nurse showed me the communal room, which had a large table and a flat-screen TV in the corner, leading to a kitchen where we would prepare our evening meals.

People were coming and going, each dealing with their own issues. I was the oldest person/patient on the ward, which was predominantly female.

I was called into the treatment room and asked to hand in any medication I had brought. I handed over a week's supply of my heart medication. I was told that I would be given any medication I needed at the appropriate times. At this point, I received my usual heart medication and my first dose of Tavor. A mental health nurse closely watched me to ensure I took the prescribed medications.

I learned that Ward 7 was one of the few wards where patients could come and go as they pleased, within reason. We were encouraged to go for walks but had to be back by 9 PM when the outer doors were locked. This freedom was because Ward 7 was for patients who had admitted themselves voluntarily, rather than being sectioned.

About half an hour after taking my first dose of Tavor, I began to feel its effects. The familiar sensation of "floating on air" set in, which I can only describe as similar to having a very strong brandy and coke. This brought a massive release of tension from my lungs, and I started to feel more at ease.

The next four hours are a blur. I sat on my bed with a million questions racing through my mind. Suddenly, my door burst open, and a young guy entered, startled to see me sitting on an extremely low bed in the corner of what he considered his room. I tried my best to explain in German who I was and why I was there.

To my relief, he started speaking perfect English, having sensed an accent in my broken German. He explained that he was studying to be an English teacher. He was super friendly and quickly pointed out that the first 24 hours in this place were the most challenging. Despite being 30 years younger than me, he made me feel at ease, or maybe it was the Tavor.

He assured me, “Stick with me, and everything will be okay.” I noticed his fingernails were painted black and, though I wondered about it, I didn’t comment. We chatted for what seemed like an eternity. When I asked why he was there, he simply said, “I have some issues in my head, I then asked about his nails, and he replied, “My girlfriend was bored!”

Soon after, he announced “Med's time”, he led me out of the room. We joined 15 other patients standing outside the treatment room, waiting for their medication. Fifteen minutes later, it was my turn. I received my usual heart medication and another Tavor tablet. My roommate then asked if I was hungry, he explained that we make our own evening meals in the well-stocked kitchen.

He also mentioned that each day, three “nominated” kitchen cleaners from Ward 7 were responsible for keeping the kitchen clean and ensuring that food was properly rotated and expired items were disposed of. It was frowned upon not to wear blue medical gloves while preparing food, which was something I had to get used to. I made myself a cheese and ham sandwich accompanied by a decaf cup of coffee.

As I sat down in the communal dining room, a young woman, maybe 23, made her appearance in an electric wheelchair. She was a ray of sunshine, greeting everyone with enthusiasm. She introduced herself to me warmly, but later confided that it was all a charade and that she hated her life.

I wanted to bring a bit of joy into her day, so I began to sing the first chorus of a familiar song, "You are my sunshine, my only sunshine." The words of the chorus flowed out softly:

"You are my sunshine, my only sunshine,
You make me happy when skies are grey.
You'll never know, dear, how much I love you.
Please don't take my sunshine away."

Even though she didn't know the words, the melody was unmistakable. It is a song that resonates deeply with many people, and she was no exception. As the familiar tune reached her ears, a small but noticeable smile crept onto her face. She looked up at me with a spark of light in her eyes and asked if I could write the song down for her.

I was more than happy to oblige. As I carefully wrote the lyrics on a piece of paper, I began to reflect on the deeper meaning behind the song. "You Are My Sunshine" is not just a simple, cheerful tune; it carries a metaphor for love and light in the midst of darkness. The opening lines, "You are my sunshine, my only sunshine" evoke a sense of warmth and comfort, symbolising a beacon of hope in the singer's life.

However, the song also harbours a profound sadness beneath its cheerful exterior. The lyrics, “I dreamed I held you in my arms / When I awoke, dear, I was mistaken,” hint at a story of love lost and a narrative of longing and heartbreak. It is a poignant reminder that while love can bring immense joy, it can also come with pain and sorrow.

As these thoughts settled in my mind, I made a decision. I didn’t want to overshadow the moment of joy with the sad parts of the song. So, I chose to omit those verses. I handed her the piece of paper with only the chorus written on it, hoping to preserve the smile I had brought to her face.

In that moment, she held onto the paper tightly, her smile growing wider. It was a small gesture, but it felt significant. The simple act of singing a song had brought a bit of sunshine into her life, if only for a brief moment.

Despite everything going on around me, I felt a sense of, “This is where I need to be.” I felt safe, thinking, “I will be fixed in a day or two.”

Feeling exhausted, I excused myself, saying it had been an exhausting and challenging day. I headed off to my room, confident that admitting myself into this stereotypical environment was the right decision. After showering in a communal shower, my roommate once again announced, “Med's time” at 10:00 PM. I received my heart medication followed by my third Tavor tablet of the day.

My roommate mentioned that he stays up every night until 2:00 AM, chatting in the corridor about his demons with a girl he met a couple of days ago. This disturbed me because I am an extremely light sleeper.

I didn't sleep well that first night because my mind was in overdrive. My roommate eventually went to bed around 2:30 AM. At one point, a stranger came into our room and spent a few seconds staring at us. The next morning, I found out it was a mental health nurse conducting a "suicide watch".

My roommate was up at 6:00 AM. He went for a shower and, upon returning, asked if he could play some music. To this day, I have no idea what was blaring out of his mobile phone.

I vaguely remembered being told there was a "roll call" every day at 7:00 AM. Gathered in one of the conference rooms and right on time, a mental health nurse entered and sat at the top of the table. He read aloud the roll call of about 15 people. When he came to my name, he introduced me to the group. Although they were present in person, their eyes seemed empty. The nurse informed us of any doctor's appointments for the day and told me I had an appointment with a psychologist later that morning. He wished us all a pleasant day and left.

My roommate then said, "Med's time". We joined the orderly queue for morning medication. After what seemed like a lifetime, I was called into the treatment room. I received my usual heart tablets and my fourth Tavor tablet in 24 hours. I mentioned my sleeping problems, and they said they would inform the doctor. I was also given a red card with my name and ward number, which I learned was for breakfast.

My roommate was waiting for me and led the way to breakfast. We walked through a maze of corridors until we reached the main building of the hospital. Along the way, he explained what various departments did.

We entered the only public restaurant in the hospital, used by doctors, nurses, visitors and everyone from Ward 7. My roommate explained the breakfast rules: we could have a boiled egg only on Sundays, and we were not allowed croissants. It was all very daunting. Essentially, we were allowed two bread rolls, some cheese, ham, or Nutella and a cup of coffee with caffeine. Everyone from Ward 7 sat at one table. After we finished, half of us walked down some stairs to the gymnasium. A young girl was waiting for us and led us through some stretching exercises for the next half hour.

Returning to my room, I took another shower. My roommate left to attend his CBT course, while I waited for my next appointment.

Looking in the mirror, I noticed my own empty stare. The Tavor tablets were making me feel numb and detached from reality, as if a barrier had formed between my mind and the outside world. My senses and emotions felt dulled by the drug's effects.

Taking this drug terrified me, but it did help calm me down. Even though the idea of using it was frightening, it was better than the alternative. The drug made me feel lifeless and detached, but it was the lesser of two evils because it brought some relief from the intense emotions and anxiety I was experiencing. My first consultation with the psychologist is a blur. He was half my age, but I at once sensed that he genuinely cared about my well-being.

During the session, I spent most of the hour in tears, gasping for air, and begging him to "make it go away". He emphasised that we could only make real progress once I was off the Devil's drug, and that this alone would take time. When the session ended, I left without fully understanding what had just happened. Then, it was time for another dose of Tavor.

In the treatment room, I met one of the senior nurses who told me she would be my dedicated mental health nurse during my stay. She spoke perfect English and mentioned she wanted to chat with me after lunch.

During our "chat," I broke down in uncontrollable tears again. What terrified me most was that I had no idea what was happening to me. I was overwhelmed by a whirlwind of emotions, both emotional and physical, and felt completely out of control. I was panic-stricken because I couldn't understand or manage the intense feelings battering me from every angle. The word, "shitty" once again was the only way that I could explain how I was feeling.

Sharing feelings of distress is really difficult, especially when those emotions are really complicated and intense. For me, saying things like "I feel shitty" or "make it stop" only start to show what I've been through, and it's something I'm still dealing with today. It's like trying to explain what it's like to be stuck in a never-ending cycle of darkness and fear.

Imagine trudging through thick mud that clings to your every step, weighing you down with each movement. Every day feels like a Herculean task, filled with exhaustion and a profound sense of heaviness. It's as if you're navigating through a dark tunnel with no glimmer of light at the end, where joy and motivation seem like distant memories.

Then there is the incessant voice in your head, whispering worst-case scenarios and fuelling a constant state of unease and dread. It's like standing on the edge of a cliff, always expecting something bad to happen. Your heart races, your palms grow clammy, and your thoughts whirl at an alarming pace, as if they're sprinting ahead faster than you can keep up.

Adding to the struggle, you bear the weight of painful memories like a heavy backpack that you can't shake off. These memories lurk in the shadows, ready to ambush you when you least expect it. When they resurface, it's like a tidal wave of emotions crashing over you, leaving you feeling defenceless and overwhelmed. It's like constantly being on edge, where even the smallest trigger can pull you back into the depths of the past.

These descriptions give you just a peek into the many feelings connected to saying things like "I feel shitty" or "make it go away." I hope I've explained what "it" means in this context.

Too Much Time on My Hands

My roommate explained that patients are usually allowed to go home on Friday or Saturday nights. However, since it was my first weekend, I had to stay in the hospital. Time seemed to stand still. With only my computer to occupy me, I must have walked at least 15 kilometres that weekend. I kept telling myself that I would be fixed soon and that my life would return to normal. I actually believed there was some sort of quick fix.

My first Friday and Saturday night in the hospital were far from quiet. The silence was repeatedly broken by the sirens of police cars and ambulances delivering what seemed like a continuous stream of screaming patients, often in handcuffs. Even after the sirens stopped, screams echoed from different parts of the hospital.

My wife and two boys visited me on Saturday evening, providing a much-needed distraction from my feelings of emptiness. It wasn't until later that they told me they barely recognised me. I was talking nonsensically and jumping from one subject to another. It was incredibly difficult for me to accept that I was in a mental hospital. I couldn't believe this was happening to me.

Finding the right words to describe how I felt was almost impossible. The fear of the unknown was overwhelming. It was like stepping into a completely unfamiliar world, one where I didn't understand the rules or know what to expect. Despite these terrifying feelings, I had a strange sense that being in the mental health hospital was necessary, which only added to my anxiety. I kept asking myself, “Why would I prefer to be here rather than at home with my wife?”

At the time, and for a long time after leaving the mental health hospital, I couldn’t answer that question. However, I believe I have addressed this painful question in the section “Why Do I Feel So ‘Shitty ’When I Have a Perfect Life?”

Looking back, the decision to admit myself into a mental health hospital was incredibly frightening at the time. I was overwhelmed with fear and anxiety about what was happening to me and what the future might hold.

However, I knew that if I didn’t take this step, “I was at risk of doing something irreversible—something I would never have the chance to regret.”

Nearly a year later, just thinking about those thoughts still sends shivers down my spine. It’s terrifying to realise how close I was to a point of no return.

The mental hospital, despite all my initial fears, became a place where I could begin to understand and address my mental health issues.

During my stay, I learned that my condition wasn’t my fault. Mental illness is like any other health condition; just as you wouldn’t blame yourself for getting the flu or breaking a bone, you shouldn’t blame yourself for having a mental health issue.

Surrounded by dedicated professionals 24 hours a day, their support was invaluable and played a significant role in my journey toward recovery.

However, despite their best intentions, I couldn't shake the feeling that they didn't fully understand the turmoil within my disillusioned, confused, and terrified mind. It was like being in a war zone of my own, far more intense and disorienting than any battlefield I had experienced before.

In an earlier chapter, I talked about being under enemy fire, with bullets whizzing past us from the right flank. That experience was undeniably frightening, but it was nothing compared to the overwhelming emotions I faced during this tough time in my life.

My understanding of mental health hospitals was shaped by the movie "One Flew Over the Cuckoo's Nest." In the film, the hospital is portrayed as a cold, sterile and oppressive institution.

The wards are stark and clinical, with a rigid daily routine enforced by authoritarian doctors and nurses. Patients have little freedom or autonomy, and the environment feels more like a prison than a place of healing. The hospital's atmosphere is tense and dehumanising, filled with power struggles and a lack of genuine care.

Contrary to the bleak depictions I'd seen in movies, my personal experience in a mental health hospital was quite different. I received compassionate care in an environment that was supportive and empowering. Throughout my stay on Ward 7, I was treated with dignity and respect, which made a significant difference in my journey towards healing.

At 10:00 PM, it was time for my medication again. This time, they gave me a new drug, 30 mg of Mirtazapine. They said it would help me sleep and work as an antidepressant.

When I was admitted, I had already been taking 25 mg of Sertraline for the past 20 days. Now, the doctor increased my dose to 50 mg. I couldn't help but think I was practically supporting the entire pharmaceutical industry. I was taking a total of 20 tablets each day—12 in the morning, 2 at midday, 4 at 6 PM, and another 2 at 10 PM.

Groundhog Day:

My first Monday morning in the mental health hospital felt almost identical to the two mornings before. Each day started with my alarm chimes at 6 AM, followed by a shower and the usual 7 o'clock roll call. On that particular Monday, I was told I had a 10 AM appointment with the lead psychiatrist and the psychologist I had spoken to on Friday. After breakfast, I joined in some sports activities, took another shower, and then waited for my appointment.

Entering the roll call room, it felt like I was walking into a job interview. The mental health professionals were seated at one end of a table, and I sat at the other end. During our meeting, I told them I felt much better and had experienced my best night's sleep in over six weeks. I was convinced I would be discharged within a week. However, they had different plans for me. They informed me that they wanted to keep me in the hospital for over six weeks, with the main goal of helping me gradually stop taking TAVOR. The lead psychiatrist explained that my current sense of improvement was due to the calming effects of TAVOR, not because I was actually getting better. I asked if it was possible to taper off TAVOR at home, hoping for a more familiar and comfortable environment. The answer was a firm "NO." They stressed that I needed to be under constant medical supervision while reducing my intake of TAVOR to ensure my safety and well-being.

The following day at roll call, I was informed that a bed had become vacant on the floor below the one I was currently on, still within Ward 7. This was undoubtedly an upgrade. The new room was significantly larger than my previous one and even had an ensuite shower.

I was to share this room with a guy who, like my first roommate, was three decades younger than me. I later discovered that he had been a patient since Christmas and had been diagnosed with severe bipolar disorder. Until then, I had heard of bipolar disorder but had limited understanding of what it truly entailed. We shared a common bond—TAVOR. My new roommate had been taking this potent medication for two years and was only now, nearly seven months after being admitted, beginning to wean off it.

Learning about his bipolar disorder motivated me to delve deeper into understanding this complex illness. I decided to research and gain a deeper understanding of the subject. As a result, I included a brief overview of bipolar disorder in the Medical Terminology section at the end of my book.

There is a vast amount of information out there, and I hope I've managed to make sense of it all. I accept that I may face criticism from medical professionals once my book is published, pointing out that certain details might not be entirely accurate. I understand their perspective; I am not trying to encroach on anyone's expertise. My aim is to break down complex medical terminology into layman's terms, making it more accessible to people like me who are trying to navigate through their own health challenges.

My time in the mental hospital seemed to drag on, with each day feeling very much the same. The only break in the monotony was that I was allowed to go home on Saturday nights. Days turned into weeks, and weeks turned into months. During that time, I couldn't see a way out of this endless cycle of struggle.

To help with my mental health issues, I was encouraged to create a schedule of activities for myself. This included long walks, sports, reading and watching movies on my computer. Although I knew these activities were meant to help me, deep down I would have preferred to sleep all day and night if given the chance.

One morning, I woke up and the stark reality hit me: I had been on Ward 7 for over five long weeks. As I inched closer to my goal of quitting TAVOR tablets, the withdrawal symptoms began to take hold, tightening their grip on my mind and body. The doctors kept reassuring me that these symptoms would eventually pass. Yet, each day felt like an eternity, and I saw no signs of relief. I felt trapped in a relentless cycle of anguish, unable to see any light at the end of the tunnel. The days blended into nights, and the torment seemed unending. My hope waned as the battle against withdrawal raged on, leaving me to wonder if I would ever emerge from this nightmare.

Everyone's experience with withdrawal symptoms from TAVOR is different. Some people may have fewer symptoms or the same ones I did, while others may face more challenging symptoms like seizures or hallucinations. What might seem like a mild side effect to one person could be life-changing for someone else. When I was going through withdrawal, I experienced symptoms like anxiety, insomnia, irritability, sweating, muscle pain, restlessness, fatigue, concentration problems, confusion, heart palpitations, depression and dizziness. There is no one-size-fits-all approach to withdrawal or to managing any health condition. What works for one person may not work for another, and what seems minor to one individual could be overwhelming to someone else. It's important to understand and respect these differences when supporting someone through withdrawal or any other medical treatment.

The realisation that each person's experience is unique has been a significant lesson for me. It's crucial to approach each situation with empathy and without assumptions. Everyone's journey is different; it was during the first three weeks that I was actually given my diagnosis.

PART V:
Diagnosis

Chapter 25

Diagnosis

Within the first two weeks of being in the mental health hospital, I was diagnosed with severe depression and anxiety. Then, during a consultation three weeks into my stay, my mental health nurse noticed signs that I was also suffering from PTSD.

While the harrowing atrocities I had seen during my time in the army undoubtedly contributed to my PTSD diagnosis. To my surprise, it was a conversation about my heart attack and three vivid, relentless memories from that event that captured the attention of my mental health nurse. These particular memories seemed to play a significant role in my diagnosis, highlighting a deeper layer of trauma beyond my wartime experiences.

During this discussion, I became engulfed in a tidal wave of emotions, my tears flowing uncontrollably as I struggled to catch my breath. The weight of reliving those haunting memories felt suffocating, leaving me with an overwhelming urge to flee the conversation and the confines of the room. Despite my distress, she insisted that we press on.

The first memory replays the scene of me lying on the floor of the surgery, surrounded by my doctor and three nurses. The air was pierced by the shrill sounds of ambulances screeching to a halt outside, a cacophony that added to the chaos and fear engulfing me in that moment.

In the second memory, I find myself clutching desperately at my GP's leg, repeatedly pleading with him to convey messages of love and apology to my wife and children that I have left without saying goodbye. The urgency in my voice echoes through the room as I insist that he go to my house and deliver these crucial words on my behalf. All the while a paramedic looms over me, brandishing what looks like an enormous needle. I feel a sense of detachment, as if I am drifting away from my body, my consciousness ebbing and flowing like the tide. Brief moments of awareness flicker in and out as I am whisked into the ambulance, only to slip into unconsciousness as my heart stops beating.

The third memory is perhaps the most emotionally charged. It's the moment when I see my wife and two boys for the first time after my heart attack. Overwhelmed with emotion, I break down in uncontrollable tears, grappling with the realisation that I might not have had the chance to express how proud I am of them and how deeply I love them.

These three memories, each carrying its own heavy emotional burden, continue to haunt me, replaying relentlessly in my mind like a broken record. What makes the torment even more unbearable is the constant barrage of chest pains, a reminder of the trauma I endured. Even now, I experience these pains multiple times a day, serving as cruel triggers that thrust me back into the depths of those harrowing memories.

Though the intensity of these thoughts may be gradually diminishing, I still grapple with chest pains on a regular basis. Despite reassurances from my heart doctor that these pains are to be expected and not a cause for alarm, they remain a constant source of distress.

I am slowly learning to navigate these waves of emotional and physical anguish, a journey that I delve into further in my book.

Without my knowledge, she informed my psychologist of her observations. Later that afternoon, I found myself sitting in front of my psychologist, taking a "PTSD" test. I failed the test drastically, ticking off nearly every symptom the psychologist mentioned.

However, there was one stark exception: I was neither physically nor verbally violent toward my family. This was a line I refused to cross, no matter the turmoil within me. Despite the relentless grip of PTSD, I held onto this boundary with unwavering resolve, determined not to let my inner demons spill over into the lives of my loved ones.

Being diagnosed with Severe Depression, Anxiety AND PTSD was like being hit by a tidal wave of fear and uncertainty. I felt utterly overwhelmed, grappling with the weight of these diagnoses that seemed to tower over me like insurmountable mountains.

I had no prior knowledge or understanding of "Mental Illnesses," and the prospect of facing them head-on felt like staring into the abyss.

Yet, amidst the chaos of my swirling emotions, there was a tiny glimmer of relief. Finally, I had names for the demons that had been haunting me, tormenting me in the shadows. They were no longer nameless spectres lurking in the darkness of my mind; they were tangible, diagnosable illnesses that I could confront, one by one.

But even with this newfound clarity, I struggled to understand the enormity of what lay ahead.

Severe Depression, Anxiety AND PTSD

Anxiety and depression are two common mental health conditions that are often talked about together, leading some people to think they always come as a package deal. However, they're actually different diagnoses, even though they can overlap quite a bit.

Anxiety is like having a constant worry or fear that something bad is going to happen. It can make you feel tense, nervous, or on edge all the time. It might even cause physical symptoms like a racing heart or sweating. On the other hand, depression is more about feeling sad, hopeless, or empty for a prolonged period.

It can zap your energy and interest in things you used to enjoy. While they're different, it's possible to have both anxiety and depression at the same time.

Imagine anxiety as always being on high alert, like you're constantly waiting for the other shoe to drop.

Depression, on the other hand, feels like being stuck in a deep, dark hole with no way out. Sometimes, these feelings can happen separately, but other times, they can team up and make things even tougher.

It's important to remember that everyone's experience is unique. Some people might have more anxiety than depression, while others might have the opposite. And just because you have one doesn't mean you're doomed to have the other.

If you're struggling with either or both, there's no shame in reaching out for help. Whether it's talking to a therapist, reaching out to friends and family, or exploring other forms of support, you don't have to go it alone.

Now, let's throw PTSD into the mix and see what happens. PTSD, or Post-Traumatic Stress Disorder, is like having a replay button stuck on your brain for a traumatic event. It can make you feel like you're reliving the experience over and over again, causing intense fear, stress, or even numbness. Now, when you add PTSD to the equation alongside anxiety and depression, it's like throwing another player into an already crowded game.

Imagine anxiety as the constant worrier, always on edge about what might happen next. Depression, on the other hand, is like a dark cloud that hangs over you, making it hard to see the sunshine.

Now, add PTSD to the mix, and it's like having flashbacks, nightmares or intrusive thoughts crashing the party when you least expect it. It can make the anxiety and depression feel even more overwhelming and complex. But here's the thing: while having all three can feel like battling a three-headed monster, it's not a life sentence.

With the right support and treatment, whether through therapy, medication, or other coping strategies, it's possible to find relief and regain control. So, if you're facing anxiety, depression, PTSD, or a combination of them all, know that you're not alone, and there's hope for brighter days ahead.

Medication Management

During my stay in the hospital, I underwent various medical checks to assess my overall health and check the effectiveness of my treatment. One of these checks included a brain MRI (magnetic resonance imaging) scan, a painless procedure that provides detailed images of the structures inside the head, primarily focusing on the brain. Thankfully, the results of the brain MRI scan yielded a sense of relief as they came back negative, showing the absence of any discernible physical neurological abnormalities.

In addition to the brain MRI, I also underwent many blood tests to evaluate various aspects of my health, including the levels of medication in my system. These blood tests were essential for checking my ongoing heart condition as well. During one of these tests, it was seen that the dosage of Sertraline I was taking, initially at 50 mg, was not providing me with its full potential as the reading was low. As a result, my healthcare team decided to increase my Sertraline dosage to 100 mg to better manage my symptoms.

Further blood tests were conducted to ensure that my Sertraline levels were within the recommended range as advised by medical experts. It was crucial to ensure that the medication was being absorbed and utilised effectively by my body to achieve the desired effect. These tests revealed that my Sertraline levels were within the green line, indicating that I was receiving an optimal dosage of the medication.

This aspect is worth highlighting as it delves into a crucial issue surrounding medication management. It is not uncommon for individuals, as I once did, to believe that increasing their medication dosage will automatically result in better symptom relief. This assumption can be misleading and potentially harmful. The truth is that the effectiveness of medication is not solely determined by the dosage; rather, it depends on various factors such as individual response, metabolism and the underlying condition being treated.

Increasing medication dosage without proper medical guidance and monitoring can pose serious risks. Not only does it fail to guarantee improved symptom relief, but it can also lead to adverse effects and other medical complications. Taking more than the prescribed amount of medication can disrupt the delicate balance within the body, potentially causing toxicity or worsening existing health issues.

Conducting regular blood tests, as in my case, can offer valuable insights into the effectiveness of the medication and help prevent unnecessary dosage adjustments.

It is worth noting that while Sertraline can be an effective treatment for various mental health conditions, including depression and anxiety, it is essential to follow the prescribed dosage guidelines. The NHS website recommends not exceeding a daily dosage of 200 mg of Sertraline. Exceeding this recommended dosage without medical supervision can increase the risk of adverse side effects and may not necessarily lead to improved treatment outcomes.

Chapter 26

Ward 7

Week five of my stay on Ward 7 marked a significant milestone in my journey toward recovery. It was during this week that I received my last dosage of TAVOR. The significance of this moment was underscored by my doctor's stern declaration: true recovery could only begin once I was free from "The Devils Drug".

Stopping TAVOR was both a relief and a new source of anxiety. While I was no longer under the drug's influence, my doctor recommended that I stay in the hospital for at least another week to monitor for any withdrawal symptoms. This cautionary advice was rooted in the unpredictable nature of benzodiazepine withdrawal, which can be both physically and mentally challenging.

Inside the hospital, I felt a strange mix of security and confinement. The environment, which often felt suffocating, also provided a sense of protection. Over the past five weeks, the intensity of my depression, anxiety and insomnia had lessened, but these issues had by no means, disappeared. The fear of these conditions returning in full force was always present, sending shivers down my spine whenever I thought about it. Adding to my anxiety was the memory of my heart attack. This traumatic experience loomed large in my mind, and the idea of having another one without immediate medical assistance was truly terrifying. The thought of dealing with such an emergency on my own was almost unbearable.

In the hospital, I felt somewhat insulated from these fears. It was as if I were wrapped in a warm, protective blanket. The presence of medical staff, the routine checks, and the constant availability of help provided a safety net that I knew I couldn't find outside the hospital walls. The hospital had become a disturbing sanctuary for me—a place I disliked being in yet depended on for my sense of security and well-being.

While I longed to leave the hospital and return to a normal life, the prospect of stepping out into the world again was daunting. The hospital had created a controlled environment where I could manage my fears and symptoms with the assurance of immediate support. Outside, I would have to face the uncertainties of life without that constant safety net.

The hospital had become both a prison and a refuge. It was a place where I felt confined yet safe, a place I wanted to leave but also needed. The journey to recovery was about more than just overcoming my mental health issues; it was also about finding a way to feel secure and resilient in the unpredictable world outside the hospital.

My Love of Art

I mentioned on the previous pages that week five of my stay on Ward 7 marked a significant milestone in my recovery journey. This was the week I received my last dosage of TAVOR. It was also the week I discovered "my love for art."

At the beginning of week five, during a consultation with my psychologist, he informed me that he had arranged a meeting with the art and design teacher later that day.

The prospect was initially intimidating. When I entered the art department, I was met with a scene that unnerved me: patients lost in their own worlds, drawing and painting in an almost eerie silence. The atmosphere felt lifeless and strange, and I quickly decided that this was not an environment I wanted to be part of. Thanking the art teacher for her time, I made my way back to my room, reflecting on my hasty decision.

Art had been something I excelled at in school, particularly O level art. This realisation prompted me to reconsider. I returned to the art department and asked the teacher for some drawing paper and a pencil. To my surprise, she generously provided me with a brand-new drawing pad, three different shades of pencils, a pencil sharpener, and an eraser.

That sunny afternoon, I walked to one of my favourite spots—a bench overlooking fields with a footpath running through the middle. For the first time, I noticed the wildflowers and bright red poppies swaying in the breeze. It was strange that I hadn't noticed the beauty of these flowers before. Sitting on the bench, I started drawing the scene in front of me. Drawing gave me a calming, relaxing feeling, and three hours passed by like half an hour.

Before heading back for my evening meal, I took many photos of the different flowers in the field. That night, during our daily call, I told my wife about my newfound hobby. I had discovered a new passion, one that transported me away from the constant stream of sadness and pain. For the rest of week five, I drew every flower in my field, each stroke of the pencil bringing me a sense of peace.

What started as a hobby soon became an obsession. I drew every free minute I had. Drawing mushroom houses became a particular refuge for me, a way to escape the "shitty" and "sad" feelings that often overwhelmed me. I drew before "roll call" after breakfast, after sports—any chance I got. What initially provided relief began to dominate my life. I would end up drawing late into the night, using it as a way to avoid my emotions.

On my regular Saturday night at home, my wife surprised me with a comprehensive art set. It included numerous pencils, watercolours, charcoal pencils, watercolour pencils and a professional drawing pad. Up until now, I had only drawn in black and white. The new materials expanded my artistic horizons, and I spent the next couple of weeks drawing what seemed like a million flowers and a hundred mushroom houses.

My drawings were well-received by my fellow patients, and even the mental health professionals requested personalised mushroom houses. While it seemed like I had found something I enjoyed, the reality was more complicated.

Every time I put pencil to paper, I knew it was an escape, an illusion to distract me from my feelings of despair.

This realisation began to terrify me. I didn't want to retreat into my drawing pad every time I felt bad. It felt like I was stuck in an ever-revolving door. (That bloody hamster wheel).

Reflecting on those early days of my new hobby, as weeks turned into months, I noticed a change. Five months after I discovered my love for art, it stopped being a means of escapism. Drawing started to bring back the joy I initially felt. I no longer used it to hide from my feelings. Instead, I wanted to draw because I enjoyed it.

I created personalised mushroom houses for my entire medical team, including my GP, therapist, dentist, friends and family. As time went on, I grew bored of drawing mushroom houses and turned my attention to some of my favourite singers—Elvis, Prince, Freddie Mercury—and iconic actors like Tom Cruise and Marilyn Monroe. Friends and family began requesting portraits of their favourite celebrities, even offering to pay for them. I started experimenting with oil paints, a new medium for me. A painting of Prince, for example, took over six weeks to complete because the oil paint took so long to dry.

As I write this book, just three days away from the one-year anniversary of my admission to the mental hospital, I only put a paintbrush to paper out of enjoyment, not as a means of escape. The journey through my mental health struggles and the discovery of my love for art have been transformative. Art has become a genuine passion, a source of joy, and an integral part of my ongoing recovery.

Elke
Elke
ONE CUP IS NOT ENOUGH

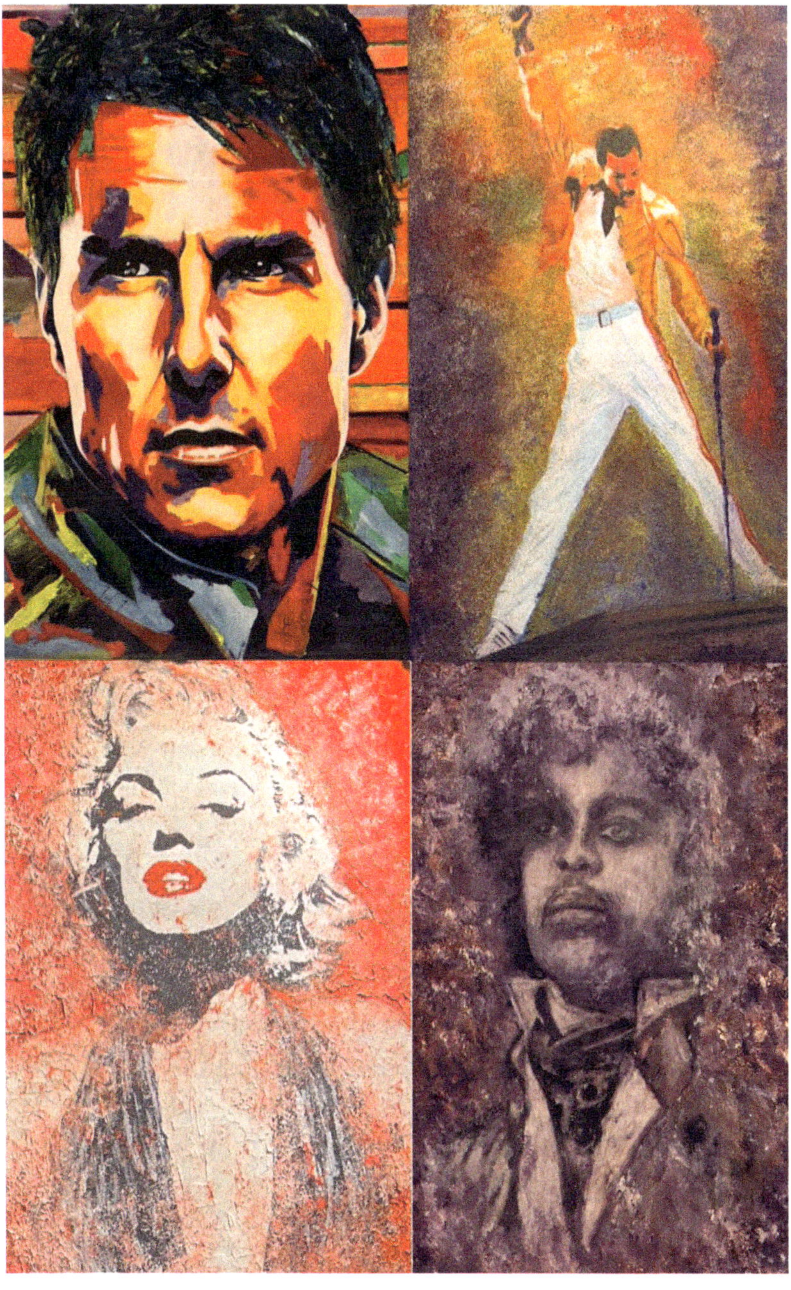

My Last Week on Ward 7.

As my final week in the mental health hospital approached, I was already aware that my psychologist would be on holiday. He confided in me that he felt guilty leaving me at such a tough time, and I could see the worry etched on his face. I reassured him that he needed to take time out for his own well-being, though the phrase "when is there ever a right time?" echoed in my thoughts.

He had promised to pass on all my notes to the chief psychiatrist before his departure, and I tried to brace myself for a slight disruption.

In the middle of my final week at the mental health hospital, things took a turn for the worse. A COVID outbreak swept through the entire hospital, affecting both patients and staff. This was soon followed by an E. coli outbreak on the ward above mine. These two events plunged us into a sudden mini lockdown.

To add fuel to the fire, the chief psychiatrist who was standing in for my psychologist contracted COVID and had to take sick leave, I felt like a ship adrift in a stormy sea.

I had a consultation with one of the hospital's doctors, someone I remembered from my admission. Together, we formulated a plan: I was considered fit enough to leave the hospital, and a comprehensive report would be sent to me at a later date. This decision seemed rushed, yet necessary, given the circumstances.

The following day, I met with a new psychologist. She was forthright with me, admitting she only had a few rough notes about my case. Despite it being no one's fault; I couldn't shake the feeling that I had been abandoned. It was as if everyone had jumped ship, leaving me to navigate the turbulent waters alone. I wasn't the only patient feeling this way; the entire ward seemed engulfed in a collective anxiety.

This sense of being sucked in and spat out sent my anxiety levels through the roof. It took a candid consultation with my mental health nurse to help me see things more clearly. We broke everything down together; it was the reality I had to face. She understood my fears of leaving the hospital and she left the decision of when to leave up to me.

I realised that my time on Ward 7 had come to an end. I felt that everything that could be done for me had been done.

On August 8, 2023, I informed my mental health nurse of my intention to leave the hospital within the next 24 hours.

Chapter 27

What causes Mental Illness?

"I don't think anyone does, I know I Don't."

My perspectives on mental illness stem not from detached observation or academic study, but rather from the raw and unfiltered chronicles of my own harrowing journey with PTSD, severe depression, and anxiety.

Throughout my experiences, I have come to realise that the actual cause of mental illness stays elusive. In my view, mental illness is not attributable to a singular factor, but rather arises from a complex interplay of hundreds of different variables.

I have come to acknowledge the intricate and sophisticated nature of mental illness, making it difficult to pinpoint a definitive cause.

Understanding that individual experiences and circumstances can vary widely.

This realisation was reinforced when I met people in the same mental hospital as myself who showed similar yet distinctly different symptoms of mental health issues. Despite sharing common diagnoses, each person's journey and manifestations of their condition were unique, highlighting the complexity and variability within mental health.

I found myself expecting simple, (sometimes, "demanding") black-and-white answers to my mental illnesses, a year later I am only now realising that this mindset was not only unrealistic but also led to frustration and misunderstandings.

Reflecting on my journey, I can't help but think that if I had known then what I know now, I could have spared myself from much pain and wasted time. Hindsight brings clarity, revealing insights and understanding that were elusive in the midst of struggle. Looking back, I see missed opportunities for seeking help, moments where I could have been kinder to myself, and paths not taken out of fear or uncertainty.

In my opinion, Mental health issues are intricately complex, shaped by a multitude of biological, environmental and psychological factors that vary significantly from person to person.

Each individual's experience is unique, and trying to oversimplify these challenges overlooks the depth and diversity of factors at play. Recognising the complexity of mental health is essential in fostering understanding, empathy, and effective approaches to support and treatment.

I now approach Mental illnesses with a holistic understanding that embraces the many factors contributing to mental illness, ranging from genetic predispositions, life experiences, trauma, environmental stressors to social and psychological influences.

Holistic Approach:

Taking a holistic approach to mental health entails recognising that mental well-being is influenced by many interconnected factors encompassing the mind, body and spirit.

Rather than focusing solely on symptoms or isolated aspects of an individual's experience, a holistic approach considers the entirety of a person's life and looks to address underlying imbalances or disruptions that may contribute to mental health challenges.

Genetic Predispositions:

In the section titled "My Sister" of my book, she highlights that genetics might influence an individual's susceptibility to certain mental health conditions.

Genetic predispositions do not guarantee the development of mental illness, however knowing that both my brother and sister have mental illness issues do suggest a genetic link.

Life experiences:

Life experiences play a crucial role in shaping mental health outcomes, influencing emotions, thoughts, behaviours, and overall well-being.

Positive experiences, such as supportive relationships, achievements, and moments of joy, can promote mental resilience and enhance psychological well-being.

Negative or traumatic experiences, such as abuse, loss, discrimination, or chronic stress, can have profound and lasting effects on mental health.

Traumatic experiences:

Drawing from my own experiences dealing with traumatic events, as detailed in the earlier pages, it becomes clear how profoundly such experiences can affect mental health. Following these traumatic events, I found myself diagnosed with post-traumatic stress disorder (PTSD), anxiety disorders, depression and grappling with various other psychological challenges.

The emotional and psychological effects of trauma showed themselves in many ways, including intrusive memories that haunted my thoughts, hyper-vigilance that left me constantly on edge, avoidance behaviours that hindered my ability to engage with the world around me and difficulties regulating my emotions, which often left me feeling overwhelmed and helpless. These symptoms not only affected my day-to-day functioning but also deeply affected my relationships, work and overall quality of life.

Environmental Stressors:

Environmental stressors may include living conditions, work-related stress, exposure to violence or discrimination, poverty, inequality and environmental degradation, financial instability, unemployment or housing insecurity, work-related stressors, such as job dissatisfaction, long hours or a hostile work environment can contribute to burnout, fatigue and mental health challenges.

Social influences:

Social factors, such as relationships, social support networks and cultural norms can also affect mental health by providing sources of resilience, validation and belonging. Strong social connections and supportive relationships can act as protective factors, buffering against stress and adversity, while social isolation or strained relationships can increase the risk of mental health issues.

Psychological influences:

Psychological influences are factors that affect how we think, feel and behave, which in turn can affect our mental health. These influences include our thought patterns, coping skills and personality traits.
I can confidently say that I have encountered nearly every aspect I'vementioned in the last 3 pages.

Stereotypes:

Despite significant strides in recognising and accepting mental illness within societies worldwide, the stigma surrounding it is still widespread.

Individuals grappling with mental health conditions often encounter derogatory labels such as "crazy," "loony," "psycho", "freak", "nuts", "weird", or "screw loose".

Despite efforts to educate and advocate, these harmful stereotypes persist, reinforcing societal misconceptions. While progress has been made, there remains a pressing need for continued awareness, empathy and support to dismantle the pervasive stigma associated with mental illness globally.

My Sister

Reflecting on the past, I can't help but wish I knew then what I know now. I'm ashamed to admit that I once used stereotypical words and phrases that I have mentioned on the previous page without fully understanding their impact. It's a regret that weighs heavy on my heart.

My sister's battle with severe depression and anxiety has been a constant presence in her life. While she may be enjoying life now, the road she's travelled has been fraught with pain and suffering. From spending weeks in mental hospitals to grappling with the relentless grip of mental illness, her journey has been nothing short of heroic.

It's only now, with a deeper understanding, empathy and first-hand experiences, that I can begin to understand the size of her struggles. My heart aches with love and admiration for her resilience and strength.

To my sister, while I may wear the visible medals of war, it is you who deserves all of them and more. Your courageous battle against depression and anxiety has been nothing short of heroic and your resilience in the face of adversity is a testament to your strength and determination. The victories you've achieved, though not recognised with tangible awards, hold far greater significance in the realm of human experience.

Your journey has only now inspired me beyond measure, and I am forever in awe of your unwavering spirit and "bollocks". You are a true warrior, and I am endlessly proud to call you, my sister.

Receiving a text from my sister recently, she posed a thought-provoking question:

"Mum also suffered with mental illness and so has our brother; do you think it's genetic? or is it life experiences? I think it's a bit of both xxxx."

Her inquiry struck a chord, prompting me to ponder the complex interplay between genetics and life experiences in shaping one's mental health. It's a question that resonates deeply as we grapple with our family's history and the challenges, we've each faced.

While the role of genetics cannot be discounted, I'm inclined to agree with her sentiment—it's likely a combination of both genetic predisposition and life's myriad experiences that contribute to the development of mental health issues. This realisation underscores the importance of holistic approaches to mental well-being.

My son's girlfriend who is studying psychology pointed out that scientists have long recognised that genes are a significant factor in most mental illnesses.

My Brother

My brother dedicated over 22 years of service to the Royal Electrical and Mechanical Engineers (REME), a testament to his unwavering commitment and expertise in his field. Throughout his distinguished career, he ascended through the ranks, culminating in his promotion to Artificer Sergeant Major (ASM), a position that speaks volumes of his leadership, technical proficiency, and the high regard in which he was held by his peers and superiors alike.

Only recently I discovered that my brother has also been grappling with PTSD and Depression. This is a personal journey that belongs to him alone. While I may have only recently become aware of his struggles, I understand that his experiences and emotions are his to share or keep private as he sees fit.

Family and Friends

The impact of mental illness on individuals extends far beyond the individual sufferer, often wreaking havoc on the lives of family and close friends.

The toll can be devastating, as loved one's grapple with the emotional turmoil and uncertainty that go with the struggles of their afflicted family member or friend.

Family members and friends may find themselves forced to prioritise their own well-being, stepping back from the chaos in an effort to preserve their own mental and emotional health.

It is a heart-breaking reality, underscoring the profound and far-reaching effects of mental illness on those who care deeply for the afflicted individual.

Mental health professionals understand the ripple effects of mental illness within families and social circles. They recognise that the impact extends beyond the individual directly experiencing the illness to encompass their loved ones as well.

Families dealing with a close friend or relative who is suffering from mental illness can face a myriad of challenges, from feelings of helplessness and frustration to strains on relationships and daily functioning.

Mental health professionals are equipped with the knowledge and expertise to provide support not only to the individual experiencing mental health issues but also to their families, offering guidance, education and coping strategies to navigate the complexities of living with and supporting someone with mental illness.

By addressing the needs of both the individual and their loved ones, mental health professionals strive to foster understanding, resilience and healing within the broader network of those affected by mental illness.

Part VI
Road to recovery

Chapter 28

Learning to ride the waves

Coping with severe depression, anxiety and PTSD has been a challenging journey for me. Over time, I've learned that these overwhelming feelings will often pass, even if it doesn't feel like it at the moment.

There are countless reasons why these feelings might ease up – from simple distractions like a phone call from a family member or completing a small task around the house to actively engaging in activities like drawing, gardening or shopping. I've found that staying active or occupied can help alleviate some of the intensity of these emotions.

While I don't want to oversimplify the experience of dealing with these feelings, I've personally found that keeping my mind occupied can be a helpful coping mechanism.

These "shitty" feelings will not completely disappear, but the strength and intensity will be alleviated. Even on days when the thoughts seem overwhelming, I've learned to ride out the waves, knowing that they will eventually pass.

Today, for example, I woke up feeling particularly down. After taking some time to write down my thoughts, I visited my local tailor at the request of my veteran friend, who needed an RCT (Royal Corps of Transport) badge sewn onto his newly purchased blazer.

Upon my return, I noticed my negative thoughts beginning to fade away, like clouds drifting across the sky.

I've realised that keeping myself busy with various activities was initially just a way to distract myself from those overwhelming feelings. Whether it was drawing, walking, gardening or simply people-watching in town, I constantly sought ways to escape the "shitty" thoughts swirling in my mind. Yet, as time passed, I began to question the purpose of it all. Was I merely going through the motions to avoid facing the reality of my emotions?

It felt like I was stuck on an endless cycle with no real meaning or fulfilment in sight. These thoughts would not go away they weighed heavily on my mind for many months.

I am thrilled to share that I can finally include this paragraph in my book with a huge sigh of relief. I've reached a point where I genuinely enjoy activities that used to feel like mere distractions. Drawing, walking and gardening have transformed from ways to pass the time into sources of genuine pleasure and fulfilment for me.

While the road to this realisation has been long and difficult, I can unequivocally say that I'm beginning to find joy and meaning in the activities that once seemed like mere coping mechanisms. This journey has taught me that sometimes, amidst the "shitty" feelings, there can be moments of genuine happiness and contentment waiting to be discovered.

Realising that I've been using the past tense more often when discussing my struggles with depression can indeed be a significant breakthrough, my, "Eurcka moment" of sorts. For example, in the above paragraph, I referred to my difficulties as "during that challenging period," showing a shift in perspective.

While acknowledging that I'm not suggesting I'm completely "fixed", this change in language usage is undoubtedly a positive sign. It suggests that I'm moving forward and beginning to distance myself from the grip of depression, recognising it as something I've faced rather than an ongoing, dominating force in my life.

This shift in language reflects a shift in mindset – a recognition of progress and resilience. You may come across the phrase, "cognitive reframing" during your journey.

My psychologist has been using this technique to help me change the way I think about a situation or problem. Instead of focusing on negative thoughts or interpretations, "cognitive reframing" encourages individuals to view things from a unique perspective, which can lead to more positive feelings and behaviours. It's like looking at a picture from a new angle to see it in a different light, helping to shift one's mindset and improve overall well-being.

While my journey may still have its ups and downs, embracing this change in perspective is a powerful step towards healing and reclaiming control over my mental health.

Good intentions.

During my time in the mental health hospital, I often received advice to "keep myself busy" and create a schedule for my activities. Even though I recognised that this guidance came from good intentions, and I knew it was beneficial, I struggled to put it into action. As someone who had admitted themselves to the hospital voluntarily, I had the freedom to leave for short periods. However, implementing the advice felt overwhelming, like facing an insurmountable obstacle. Despite understanding the importance of staying occupied, the task seemed daunting and difficult to carry out.

Even the simplest tasks felt overwhelming during that tough time in my life. Shaving, showering, going for a walk and even eating seemed like monumental challenges. If I could have, I would have slept all day just to avoid facing the reality of my struggles. I remember spending countless hours lying in bed, consumed by feelings of despair and hopelessness.

I wish I could provide a straightforward explanation of how I managed to navigate through this tumultuous period, but the truth is, there isn't one. While I can offer some recommendations based on my own experience with treatment, there's no one-size-fits-all solution. Coping with depression and mental health challenges is a complex journey that requires time and patience. However, I am living proof that things can and do get better with time and perseverance.

In the next three chapters, I delve into Cognitive-Behavioural Therapy, Mindfulness, and Meditation—three subjects that have been, and continue to be, valuable tools in my recovery journey.

Chapter 29

Thoughts and Feelings Toolbox

Cognitive-behavioural therapy (CBT). As I like to call it, "Thoughts and Feelings Toolbox" (TFT), can indeed seem overwhelming at first, especially with all the information out there. But think of it like a toolbox packed with practical equipment to help us navigate our thoughts and emotions more effectively.

In essence, CBT teaches us to recognise the connection between our thoughts, feelings and actions and equips us with strategies to intervene positively in this cycle. It's like having a set of reliable implements at our disposal to tackle challenges and promote mental well-being.

Imagine each piece of equipment in the CBT toolbox as a specific technique designed to address various aspects of our mental health. For example, one tool might help us identify and challenge negative thought patterns, while another might focus on managing overwhelming emotions.

By learning and practicing these techniques, we can gradually build our resilience and cope better with life's ups and downs. Rather than feeling lost in a sea of information, CBT empowers us to take an active role in our mental health journey.

So, in a nutshell, CBT stands for Cognitive Behavioural Therapy, which is a type of therapy that helps people understand how their thoughts, feelings and behaviours are connected. It's like training your brain to recognise and change unhelpful thinking patterns or habits that might be causing stress, anxiety or other problems.

Instead of just talking about feelings, CBT gives you practical tools to challenge negative thoughts and learn new, healthier ways of coping with life's ups and downs. It's all about taking control of your mind and building skills to feel better and live more confidently.

1. Thinking: CBT helps us understand that our thoughts can affect how we feel. For example, if we keep thinking, "I'm not good enough," we might start feeling sad or worried. CBT teaches us to notice these negative thoughts and challenge them by finding evidence that they might not be true.

2. Feeling: Our thoughts can make us feel different emotions. CBT teaches us ways to change our thoughts to feel better. For instance, if we're feeling scared about a test, we can learn to think more positively, like studied hard, so I'll do my best."

3. Doing: CBT also looks at how our actions are connected to our thoughts and feelings. If we're feeling anxious about making new friends, we might avoid talking to people. CBT helps us face our fears gradually and learn that we can handle situations better than we thought.

In CBT, a therapist helps us understand these connections and teaches us skills to challenge negative thoughts, manage tough emotions and change behaviours that aren't helpful. It's like learning how to use tools to fix problems in our minds, so we can feel happier and more confident in our lives.

My introduction to Cognitive Behavioural Therapy (CBT) came unexpectedly during my time in a mental health hospital, an experience I share in the chapter detailing my admission.

Choosing to admit myself into Gilead 4, a mental health hospital in Bielefeld, meant living on a ward that wasn't under constant lock-down. This freedom allowed for short excursions, like walks or trips to the shops, although returning by 9 PM was mandatory. On the ward, there was a noticeable division among patients. While some were enrolled in an intensive 9-week live-in CBT course, I found myself categorised as a "Crisis" patient.

During the first four weeks, the concept of CBT remained a mystery to me. It wasn't until I took matters into my own hands and delved into research that I began to unravel the intricacies of CBT. This newfound understanding shed light on the therapeutic approach that many of my fellow patients were undergoing.

Chapter 30

Mindfulness

Mindfulness is a mental practice that involves being fully present and engaged in the moment, without judgment. It's like giving your full attention to whatever you're doing, whether it's eating, walking or even just breathing. It's about being aware of your thoughts, feelings, bodily sensations and the environment around you, without getting caught up in them or reacting to them automatically.

At its core, mindfulness is about cultivating awareness and acceptance of the present moment. It's about noticing what's happening right now, both inside and outside of you, without getting lost in regrets about the past or worries about the future.

Practicing mindfulness can involve various techniques such as meditation, breathing exercises, or simply paying attention to your senses. It's not about emptying your mind of thoughts but rather seeing them without getting carried away by them.

One key aspect of mindfulness is non-judgmental awareness. Instead of labelling experiences as good or bad, right or wrong, mindfulness encourages you to see them with curiosity and openness. This attitude of acceptance can help reduce stress, anxiety and overthinking something, allowing you to respond to life's challenges with greater clarity and calmness.

So, in a nutshell - Mindfulness is like giving your brain a break from all the noise and distractions, and instead, focusing on what's happening right now, whether it's your breath, your thoughts, or what you're doing. It's about being fully aware and accepting of the present moment, without getting caught up in your thoughts. It's a way to find tranquillity and peacefulness in the midst of everyday chaos.

Ten tips to help you practice mindfulness:

1. Start with the breath: Focus on your breath as it enters and leaves your body. Notice the sensation of each inhale and exhale, bringing your attention back to your breath whenever your mind starts to wander.

2. Practice regularly: Set aside time each day to engage in mindfulness exercises, even if it's just for a few minutes. Consistency is key to developing mindfulness habit.

3. Be present: Pay attention to the present moment without judgment. Notice the sights, sounds, smells and sensations around you, fully immersing yourself in the here and now.

4. Use your senses: Engage your senses to anchor yourself in the present moment. Notice the textures, colours and shapes of objects, as well as any sounds or smells in your environment.

5. Accept your thoughts and feelings: Instead of trying to suppress or control your thoughts and emotions, practice accepting them without judgment. Allow them to come and go like clouds passing in the sky.

6. Practice non-reactivity: When faced with challenging thoughts or emotions, observe them without reacting impulsively. Take a step back and respond mindfully, rather than letting your emotions dictate your actions.

7. Be kind to yourself: Treat yourself with compassion and kindness, especially when you're struggling. Practice self-care and self-compassion, acknowledging that it's okay to make mistakes and to be imperfect.

8. Engage in mindful activities: Incorporate mindfulness into everyday activities such as eating, walking, or even washing dishes. Pay attention to each moment and savour the experience fully.

9. Cultivate gratitude: Take time to appreciate the positive aspects of your life, no matter how small. Reflect on what you're grateful for and express appreciation for the people and things that bring you joy.

10. Be patient: Remember that mindfulness is a skill that takes time to develop. Be patient with yourself and trust in the process, knowing that each moment of mindful awareness contributes to your overall well-being.

Finding the right tools for mindfulness can make an enormous difference in your daily routine. Personally, I've experimented with various apps and meditation videos, but only two have stuck with me. When I need a quick moment of mindfulness on the go, my go-to is my Apple Watch, which offers short mindfulness exercises. For longer, more immersive sessions, I rely on a free app called Smiling Mind. It provides guided meditations and mindfulness exercises that help me unwind and recharge, especially during those longer, uninterrupted moments, like when I'm relaxing in the bath. Integrating these practices into my daily life has become a soothing ritual that helps me stay grounded.

Chapter 31

Breathing Technique

Box breathing technique, also known as square breathing, is a simple and effective breathing exercise that can help calm the mind, reduce stress and improve focus. It involves breathing in a structured manner, typically in four equal parts:

1. Inhale: Breathe in slowly and deeply through your nose for a count of four.

2. Hold: Hold your breath for a count of four.

3. Exhale: Breathe out slowly through your mouth for a count of four.

4. Hold: Hold your breath again for a count of four before repeating the cycle.

If the box breathing technique feels a bit challenging, try this simpler method:

1. "Breath in, two, three, four."

2. "Hold, two, three, four."

3. "Breath out, two, three, four, five, six."

Chapter 32

Meditation

My Journey with Meditation. I am writing this chapter exactly one year ago to the day since I admitted myself into a mental health hospital.

I used to think meditation was for "weird" people—those "space cadets" and "hippies" who seemed out of touch with reality. I never imagined that meditation would become a tool in my recovery journey.

Meditation is a practice that helps you relax and calm your mind. It involves sitting quietly, usually with your eyes closed and focusing on your breathing or repeating a soothing word or phrase.

An important part of meditation is being aware of your breath, something I used to take for granted. This hit home during a visit to the dentist, which I hate. My eldest son was with me and calmly said, "Dad, breathe". I had forgotten to breathe! I closed my eyes, took several deep breaths, letting my stomach rise and fall, and it helped me calm down.

When I left the mental health hospital, I knew I needed to stay both physically and mentally active to aid my recovery. That's when I subscribed to Apple Fitness+. The service made it easy and fun to do workouts at home.

In addition to physical workouts, Apple Fitness+ also offers hundreds of meditation exercises. These range from beginner to advanced levels, the sessions felt very personal, almost like having a one-on-one session with a coach. The quality of these sessions impressed me so much that I cannot help but recommend Apple's service, despite not having any affiliation with the company.

By chance, I stumbled upon an app called Smiling Mind. This app, which is free and remarkably user-friendly, focuses on mindfulness and meditation. To my surprise, I found myself using Smiling Mind more often than Apple Fitness+.

The main reason for this switch was how Smiling Mind enhanced my meditation practice. With Apple Fitness+ meditation sessions, I often kept my eyes open, which caused my mind to wander more easily. However, with Smiling Mind, I have no choice but to close my eyes, making it much easier to concentrate on the meditation exercises. This small but significant difference helped me stay focused and achieve a deeper sense of calm during my sessions.

My preferred spot for a 20-minute meditation session is in my bath filled with stress-relief salts. There, I can feel my breath's inhales and exhales more distinctly.

While I have made considerable progress with my mental well-being, my physical health has taken a back seat. Since leaving the mental hospital, I've gained 20kg. I often tell myself that this weight gain is a side effect of my medication, and while that may be partly true, I know I need to do more to stay physically active.

I try to go for a half-hour walk every day and stay active with house and garden work. However, these efforts aren't enough. Recently, I found out that I'm within the pre-diabetes range, which means I need to cut down on sugary treats and take my physical health more seriously.

PART VII:
My advice

Chapter 33

Mental Illness is a medical condition

Mental illness is like any other health condition; it's not your fault if you're experiencing it. Just as you wouldn't blame yourself for getting the flu or breaking a bone, you shouldn't blame yourself for having a mental health issue.

These conditions are complex and can be caused by a variety of factors, including genetics, brain chemistry, life experiences and stress.

Blaming yourself can be harmful because it can lead to feelings of low self-esteem, guilt and depression, (which only makes matters worse) and it can also prevent individuals from seeking help or support when they need it.

It's common to have feelings of, "Self-Blame" when we're unsure about what caused a negative outcome. It's like searching for answers in a foggy landscape, where clarity seems out of reach.

During such times, we may feel overwhelmed by a sense of helplessness, like we're stuck in a situation we can't change. This combination of uncertainty and powerlessness can weigh heavily on our minds, leading to feelings of frustration and distress.

It's important to remember that it's okay to not have all the answers. When we experience self-blame and feelings of powerlessness, it's like being caught in a storm without an umbrella. We may feel exposed and vulnerable, unable to shield ourselves from the onslaught of negative thoughts and emotions. It's crucial to recognise that these feelings are natural responses to challenging situations and that we're not alone in experiencing them.

Encouraging open conversations about mental health can foster understanding and break down the stigma that often surrounds these conditions.

It's essential for everyone to know that seeking help is a sign of strength, not weakness.

Whether it's therapy, medication, or lifestyle changes, there are effective treatments available that can make a significant difference.

By promoting a supportive environment, we can make it easier for those struggling to step forward and access the care they need, contributing to healthier individuals and communities.

I'm grateful for the opportunity to share my journey with you.

Chapter 34

Dealing with mental health issues

Dealing with mental health issues can be challenging, but there are steps you can take to get help and support. Here is my advice:

1. Talk to a Family Member or Close Friend: Sharing your feelings with someone you trust can provide comfort and understanding. Don't hesitate to reach out to those close to you.

2. Seek Professional Help: It's important to consult with a medical professional, such as a GP (General Practitioner) or a mental health specialist. They can provide a proper diagnosis and recommend the best course of action.

3. Consider Antidepressant Medication for example: Sertraline*/Mirtazapine** When you consult with your GP or mental health professional, discuss the possibility of taking antidepressant medication.

4. Just as you might take painkillers for physical pain, antidepressants can help ease the symptoms of depression. This advice is personal and may not be suitable for everyone, so it's important to have a thorough discussion with your doctor.

5. Seek Therapy: Therapy can be a powerful tool in managing mental health issues. Therapists can offer strategies and support to help you navigate your feelings and challenges.

6. Educate Yourself: Empower yourself with correct, up-to-date information. The NHS website is a great place to start for reliable information on mental health. Understanding more about your condition can help you make informed decisions about your treatment and care.

Remember, reaching out for help is a courageous and important first step towards recovery. There are many resources and people ready to support you through this journey.

***Sertraline**

I have been taking 100mg a day at 8 AM for nearly a year. Sertraline (Zoloft), a commonly prescribed Selective serotonin reuptake inhibitor (SSRI) for depression, anxiety and other mood disorders.

Some of the common side effects <u>may</u> include:

More common:

- Decreased interest in sexual intercourse
- failure to discharge semen

- inability to have or keep an erection
- loss in sexual ability, desire, drive, or performance

Less common or rare:

- Aggressive reaction
- breast tenderness or enlargement
- confusion
- diarrhoea
- drowsiness
- dryness of the mouth
- fast talking and excited feelings or actions that are out of control
- fever
- inability to sit still
- increase in body movements
- increased sweating
- increased thirst

- lack of energy
- loss of bladder control
- mood or behaviour changes
- muscle spasm or jerking of all extremities
- nosebleeds
- overactive reflexes
- racing heartbeat
- red or purple spots on the skin
- restlessness
- seizures
- shivering
- skin rash, hives, or itching
- sudden loss of consciousness
- unusual or sudden body or facial movements or postures
- unusual secretion of milk (in females)

****Mirtazapine**

I was taking 30mg until I was raised to 45mg a day at 10 PM for nearly a year. Mirtazapine is an antidepressant that works by affecting neurotransmitters in the brain. While it is not a sleeping tablet, it can make you feel sleepy, which can be helpful if you have depression and difficulties getting to sleep.

Some of the side effects may include:

More common:

- Constipation
- dizziness
- drowsiness
- dry mouth
- increased appetite
- weight gain

Less common:

- Abnormal dreams
- back pain

- dizziness or fainting when getting up suddenly from a lying or sitting position
- increased need to urinate
- increased sensitivity to touch
- increased thirst
- low blood pressure
- muscle pain
- nausea
- sense of constant movement of self or surroundings
- stomach pain
- trembling or shaking
- vomiting

Side effects can vary in intensity and duration, and not everyone will experience them.

It is important to discuss any concerns or persistent side effects with a healthcare provider. I can't stress enough the importance of doing your research. I only discovered what the side effects are from taking Sertraline and Mirtazapine six months after my initial dose.

Treatment

Treatment for mental illness offers a beacon of hope, often serving as a lifeline for those grappling with its formidable grip. However, it is crucial to dispel any illusions of quick fixes or instant remedies. Finding the right treatment is a journey fraught with challenges and setbacks, one that requires patience, perseverance, and above all, TIME.

Mental illness defies simple solutions; The road to recovery is riddled with obstacles, and there are no shortcuts or easy answers.

Among the struggle, there exists a community of millions who understand the depth of your pain and share in your journey.

While the journey may be arduous, there is solace in knowing that you are not alone, that there are others who have weathered similar storms and emerged stronger for it. Together, we learn to navigate the turbulent waters of mental illness, riding the waves of despair with resilience and determination, refusing to let the darkness consume us.

It's imperative to recognise that help and support for mental illness is available, and suffering in silence should never be a choice. Taking the courageous step to open up about your struggles, whether to a family member, friend, or mental health professional, can be a transformative act in itself.

Simply sharing your experiences and emotions with someone you trust can alleviate the burden of isolation and provide a sense of relief. Sometimes the simple act of verbalising your thoughts and feelings can be a crucial first step on the path towards healing and recovery.

Remember, you are not alone, and there are people who care about you and are willing to offer the support and understanding you need to navigate the challenges of mental illness.

It's essential to approach mental health treatment with caution and awareness, as different professionals may employ vastly different methods and approaches.

Unlike many physical ailments with standardised treatment protocols, mental illnesses present a complex landscape with a multitude of remedies and medications available to practitioners.

First-hand experiences highlight the potential pitfalls of blindly accepting treatment recommendations, as shown by encounters with medications like Tavor.

My own experience with this drug serves as a cautionary tale, as I unwittingly became addicted to its effects, ultimately leading to a breakdown and hospitalisation.

This underscores the importance of conducting thorough research and taking an active role in one's own treatment journey.

While the guidance of professionals is invaluable, it's essential to remain vigilant and informed, using resources like the internet responsibly to empower oneself with knowledge and advocate for the most effective and proper care.

As more and more individuals recognise the importance of seeking professional help for mental health issues, actually finding professional help can take TIME.

Finding the courage to reach out for help is a crucial first step, but it's just the beginning of a journey that may be fraught with challenges and setbacks.

The process of finding the right treatment can be time-consuming and stressful, worsening feelings of anxiety and uncertainty.

It's natural to question the point of it all, I implore you to stop those destructive thoughts in their tracks. I am living proof that recovery—or at least a reduction in the intensity of those debilitating feelings—is not only possible but achievable.

For those fortunate enough to have a support system of family and friends, I urge you to lean on them, to share your burdens and seek solace in their presence.

However, from my own experience, I recommend against turning to chat rooms or online forums, as they can sometimes do more harm than good.

If you ever find yourself on the brink of despair, thinking about doing something to make, "it all go away" I urge you to stop and take a deep breath. Please reach out for help right away, whether that means calling a dedicated 24-hour helpline or seeking medical help.

There is hope, even in the darkest of moments and with the right support and guidance, you can navigate the turbulent waters of mental illness and emerge stronger on the other side.

Panic attacks

Since my heart attack, I've encountered many panic attacks and the first one was undeniably the most terrifying. Panic attacks are truly frightening; during that initial episode, I was convinced I was experiencing another heart attack.

In the midst of my panic attack, I was in a dark place mentally, still wrestling with the grip of my PTSD, severe depression and anxiety. Despite the seriousness of the situation, when my wife urged me to call an ambulance, I hesitated.

The overwhelming fear of reliving the traumatic experiences from my earlier heart attack held me back. In that tense moment, I was so consumed by fear and uncertainty that I refused to consider calling for help until I was absolutely certain I was experiencing another heart attack. However, even in the midst of my turmoil, I failed to recognise how remarkably composed my wife remained. It was as if she intuitively understood that panicking would only exacerbate the situation, and her calm demeanour provided a sense of stability in the midst of chaos.

The panic attack struck while I was out with my wife and some friends in a restaurant. Suddenly, without any warning or obvious triggers, I felt my heart racing, struggled to catch my breath, and was gripped by chest pains.

The situation worsened when my Apple Watch indicated that my heart was in Atrial fibrillation, heightening my sense of panic. Upon returning home, I was in a dire state. Checking my blood pressure revealed a troubling reading of 200/120, adding to my distress.

At that time, I wasn't prepared for having a panic attack. I only wish I knew then what I know now about managing such episodes (I've mentioned this so many times throughout my book).

During the attack, I lay down on my bed, feeling overwhelmed and unsure of what to do. In an attempt to calm myself, I started taking deep, regular breaths as I focused on my breathing, I imagined something comforting: eating a Cornish pasty while watching the waves crash on the Cornish shore.

This visualisation, combined with the deep breathing, really helped to calm me down. Gradually, I felt my symptoms begin to subside. By creating a peaceful mental image and controlling my breathing, I was able to manage the panic attack more effectively.

The impact of that first panic attack lingered long after the symptoms had subsided. I found myself compulsively checking my blood pressure multiple times a day, incessantly checking my pulse and even taking more than twenty ECGs a day on my Apple Watch in a desperate attempt to regain a sense of control. However, as time passed, I began to recognise that these constant health checks only served to worsen my anxiety, fuelling a cycle of fear and apprehension. In hindsight, I realise that these medical gadgets, while intended to provide reassurance, often had the opposite effect, amplifying my worries and perpetuating a state of heightened vigilance. Looking back, I now wish I had discarded them altogether, understanding that true healing comes from within rather than from external measurements or reassurances.

Knowing how to respond during a panic attack, whether it's happening to you or someone you care about, is crucial.

It's important to stay calm. Whether you're experiencing the panic attack yourself or you're supporting a family member or friend, keeping a sense of calm can help to prevent the situation from escalating. Panic attacks are frightening, but staying composed can provide reassurance and stability during a challenging moment (easier said than done - I know).

Focusing on your breathing is essential during a panic attack. Many people tend to hyperventilate, gasping for air, which can worsen the symptoms.

It's important to breathe deeply. I use the Box Breathing Technique. Make sure you feel your stomach inflate with each breath, similar to blowing up a balloon. Repeat this process until you feel more relaxed, then return to your normal breathing pattern. I've personally found that practicing this technique daily has significantly reduced my stress levels over time.

Remind yourself that the attack will pass and try to focus on peaceful, relaxing images. I imagine myself in Looe, Cornwall, eating a Cornish pasty while watching the crashing waves.

10 tips to help you during a panic attack:

1. Practice deep breathing: (Square breathing technique) Take slow, deep breaths to help calm your body and mind.

2. Focus on the present: Try to ground yourself by focusing on your surroundings or a specific object.

3. Use calming self-talk: Remind yourself that the panic attack will pass and that you are safe.

4. Progressive muscle relaxation: Tense and then relax each muscle group in your body to release tension.

5. Reach out for support: If possible, talk to someone you trust or call a helpline for support.

6. Consider therapy: Cognitive-behavioural therapy (CBT) or other therapies can help you manage panic attacks in the long term.

7. Avoid caffeine and alcohol: These substances can worsen anxiety and trigger panic attacks.

8. Practice mindfulness or meditation: Regular mindfulness practices can help reduce overall anxiety levels.

9. Stay hydrated and eat balanced meals: Proper nutrition can support your overall well-being.

10. Know your triggers: Understanding what triggers your panic attacks can help you avoid or manage them more effectively.

Hypertension

Understanding Hypertension: The Silent Threat

Hypertension, commonly known as high blood pressure, is a condition where the force of blood against the walls of the arteries is consistently too high. It's often called the "silent killer" because it typically has no symptoms but can lead to serious health complications if left untreated. Let's dive into what hypertension is, its causes, symptoms and how it can be managed.

What is Hypertension?

Blood pressure is the measurement of the force exerted by blood against the walls of the arteries as it flows through the body. It's recorded as two numbers: systolic pressure (the pressure when the heart beats) and diastolic pressure (the pressure when the heart is at rest between beats). A blood pressure reading of 120/80 mm Hg is considered normal, while readings consistently higher than this indicates hypertension.

Causes of Hypertension

Hypertension can be caused by a range of factors, including:

1. Unhealthy Lifestyle: Poor diet, lack of exercise, smoking and excessive alcohol consumption can all contribute to high blood pressure.

2. Genetics: A family history of hypertension can increase the risk of developing the condition.

3. Age: Blood pressure tends to rise with age due to changes in the arteries and blood vessels.

4. Underlying Health Conditions: Conditions such as kidney disease, thyroid disorders and sleep apnoea can contribute to hypertension.

5. Stress: Chronic stress can temporarily raise blood pressure and, over time, contribute to hypertension.

Symptoms of Hypertension

In most cases, hypertension doesn't cause noticeable symptoms until it reaches a severe stage. Some people may experience headaches, shortness of breath, nosebleeds or dizziness, but these symptoms are not specific to hypertension and can be caused by other factors. That's why regular blood pressure screenings are crucial for early detection.

Complications of Hypertension

If left untreated, hypertension can lead to serious health complications, including:

1. Heart Disease: High blood pressure can damage the arteries, increasing the risk of heart attack, stroke and other cardiovascular diseases.

2. Kidney Damage: The kidneys play a crucial role in regulating blood pressure. Hypertension can damage the blood vessels in the kidneys, leading to kidney failure or kidney disease.

3. Eye Problems: High blood pressure can damage the blood vessels in the eyes, leading to vision problems or even blindness.

4. Aneurysm: The constant pressure of blood flow against weakened arteries can cause them to balloon and form an aneurysm, which can rupture and be life-threatening.

Managing Hypertension

Fortunately, hypertension can be managed effectively with lifestyle changes and if necessary, medication.

Here are some strategies for managing hypertension:

1. Healthy Diet: Eat a balanced diet rich in fruits, vegetables, whole grains, lean proteins and low-fat dairy products. Limit salt, saturated fats and refined sugars.

2. Regular Exercise: Aim for at least 30 minutes of moderate intensity exercise most days of the week. This can help lower blood pressure and improve overall cardiovascular health.

3. Maintain a Healthy Weight: Losing excess weight can help lower blood pressure. Even a modest weight loss can make a significant difference.

4. Limit Alcohol and Quit Smoking: Limit alcohol consumption to moderate levels and avoid smoking altogether.

5. Manage Stress: Practice relaxation techniques such as deep breathing, meditation, or yoga to help manage stress and lower blood pressure.

6. Medication: If lifestyle changes alone are not enough to control hypertension, your doctor may prescribe medication to help lower blood pressure.

It’s essential to take medication as prescribed and attend regular check-ups to check blood pressure levels.

Conclusion

Hypertension is a common but serious condition that affects millions of people worldwide. While it often goes unnoticed due to its lack of symptoms, untreated hypertension can lead to severe health complications. By making healthy lifestyle choices and seeking proper medical care, hypertension can be effectively managed, reducing the risk of complications and improving overall health and well-being. Regular blood pressure screenings are key to early detection and treatment, so don’t hesitate to talk to your healthcare provider if you have concerns about your blood pressure.

Chapter 35

"Shitty - Sad"

In my personal journey with severe depression, anxiety and PTSD, I often struggle to put my feelings into words.

In my attempts to express myself, I've used simple terms like "shitty" and "sad" to describe the depth of my emotions. Even now, it's challenging for me to articulate the full extent of what I mean by these words.

When I say I feel "shitty," I'm trying to convey the overwhelming sense of heaviness and emptiness that weighs me down. It's like carrying a burden that never seems to lighten, no matter how hard I try to shake it off. Everything feels bleak and hopeless, and it's hard to find joy or meaning in anything.

Similarly, when I say I feel "sad," it goes beyond just feeling down or blue. It's a profound sadness that consumes me, making it difficult to see beyond the darkness. It's like being trapped in a deep, dark hole with no way out, suffocating under the weight of my own despair.

Simple triggers, like hearing sad news stories or seeing my dogs looking sombre, can provoke intense emotional responses. Even seemingly ordinary events, such as a friend mentioning their pet's trip to the vet, can unexpectedly lead to uncontrollable tears.

My journey with mental health struggles has taught me that emotions don't always follow a logical pattern.

While these words may seem simplistic, they hold immense power in capturing the complex emotions I experience. They serve as a reminder that mental illness is not always easy to describe or understand, but it's real and it's valid. And even though finding the right words may be a struggle, I know that expressing my feelings, however imperfectly, is an important step towards healing and recovery.

Why Do I Feel So Shitty, when I Have a Perfect Life?

Often, I found myself repeatedly asking this question to my psychologist, psychiatrist and myself, seeking understanding and relief from my emotional pain.

On the other hand, have you ever wondered why a family member or a friend with a seemingly perfect life can still feel overwhelmingly, "shitty" all the time?

It's a question many well-meaning friends and family members may ask when they see a loved one struggling with depression. They might say, "But you have everything going for you! Why can't you just be happy?"

The truth is depression isn't just about feeling sad in response to specific events or circumstances.

When it's described as "a complex mental health condition characterised by biochemical and physical abnormalities in the brain," it means that the illness involves changes or disruptions in the chemical and physical processes of the brain.

These changes can lead to various symptoms, such as changes in mood, difficulty thinking clearly or altered perception of reality.

Essentially, it highlights that mental illness involves not just psychological factors, but also biological factors related to the functioning of the brain.

Imagine waking up each day with a heavy weight on your chest, feeling like there's no fun or meaning in anything you do. That's what it's like for many people living with depression. It's not a matter of simply "snapping out of it" or "thinking positively". The sadness and hopelessness they experience are very real and can be incredibly overwhelming.

For someone with depression, being told to "just be happy" or that they have no reason to be sad can feel dismissive and frustrating. It's like telling someone with a broken leg to just walk it off – it's not that simple.

Finding Joy in the Ups and Downs of Life

Life is a journey filled with twists and turns, highs and lows, laughter and tears. Reflecting on my early years, it's undeniable that sadness has been a frequent visitor.

However, despite the challenges and hardships, I wouldn't trade my life for anything in the world.

The reason is simple: amidst the sorrow, there have been countless moments of joy and triumph that have shaped me into the person I am today.

Growing up, I encountered my fair share of struggles. From family hardships to personal setbacks, each obstacle seemed to weigh heavily on my young shoulders.

There were moments when despair threatened to consume me, and it would have been easy to succumb to bitterness and resentment. Yet, even in the darkest of times, I clung to the flicker of hope that burned within me.

It's true that my journey has been marked by both ups and downs. But for every setback I faced, there were countless victories waiting to be celebrated. Whether it was overcoming adversity, achieving personal milestones, or simply finding moments of pure happiness, these experiences served as beacons of light in the darkness.

One of the most remarkable aspects of my life is the resilience and strength that I've discovered within myself. Each trial I've endured has only served to make me stronger, more resilient and more determined to pursue my dreams. Rather than allowing adversity to defeat me, I've used it as fuel to propel myself forward.

But perhaps the greatest gift that life has given me is the ability to find joy in the most unexpected places. Despite the pain and sadness that have punctuated my journey, I've always managed to find reasons to smile.

Whether it's sharing a laugh with loved ones, pursuing my passions, or simply revelling in the beauty of the world around me, I've learned to cherish the moments of happiness that life offers.

So, while my early years may have been marked by sadness, I wouldn't change a single moment of it. For it is through adversity that I've discovered my strength, through hardship that I've learned to appreciate the beauty of life, and through sorrow that I've found moments of unparalleled joy. The ups far outweigh the downs. And as I continue my journey, I look forward to sharing the laughter, the tears and the countless moments of joy that lie ahead.

It's difficult to name someone who hasn't experienced ups and downs in life, as these fluctuations are inherent to the human experience.

While some may appear to have smoother journeys than others, it's important to recognise that everyone faces their own unique set of challenges and hardships.

Comparing one's struggles to those of others can be a humbling reminder that adversity manifests in various forms, and what may seem like a minor setback to one person could be a monumental obstacle to another.

Acknowledging that others have endured far greater hardships serves as a reminder of resilience and the capacity for strength in the face of adversity.

Chapter 36

Poor Mental Health or Mental Illness?

Distinguishing between mental illness and episodes of poor mental health is a challenge many of us face, but it's an essential one to tackle. Poor mental health often stems from temporary fluctuations in mood or well-being, like passing clouds in the sky.

While we all experience periods of poor mental health, characterised by feelings of sadness, distress, anxiety, or even depression-like symptoms, these are often situation-specific and time-limited. Challenges such as relationship breakdowns, job loss, bereavement, or financial difficulties can indeed feel overwhelming, but typically, with time and support, they tend to improve.

However, with my personal experience dealing with severe depression, anxiety and PTSD which involved more enduring and severe disturbances in thoughts, emotions, or behaviours that significantly affected my ability to function in daily life.

At the time I had no idea what was going on. I just wanted it to, "go away" by, "any means necessary".

These conditions didn't just come and go like passing storms; they lingered, clouding every aspect of my life, and making even the simplest tasks feel like climbing mountains. At the time, I was desperate for relief but finding it on my own proved impossible. It was only through seeking professional medical help that I began to find my way out of the darkness.

It's crucial not to downplay the distress caused by situational challenges, but it's equally important to recognise the profound impact of mental illness. By acknowledging the differences between these experiences, we can better understand our own mental health and support others who may be struggling.

Get your house in order

"Get your house in order" – this doesn't mean cleaning behind that piece of furniture you've neglected for over five years.

One of my biggest regrets was not getting my house in order. During my heart attack, countless thoughts raced through my mind—things I wished I had said but never found the time or felt the urgency to express.

I urge you to take a moment, grab a coffee, and reflect. If you were to leave this world today, what regrets would you carry with you?

Even though I repeatedly told my wife and two boys that I loved them, looking back, it felt like something I said out of routine. I truly meant it, but I hadn't conveyed how deeply I love them or how proud I am of them. Don't overdo it but take the time to genuinely express your feelings. Life is too short to hold grudges. If you've had a falling out with family or friends, take the first step to mend those relationships. You'll feel better for it.

Consider this: if you lost a family member or a friend, would you find yourself saying, "I only wish I had done or said that?"

Also, think about this: if you were to leave now, would your partner know what to do? In relationships, we often have different responsibilities.

To make things easier for your loved ones, jot down valuable information only you know. Write down your phone's PIN, banking passwords, the name of your bank, where you keep your passports, and so on. If you leave this world unexpectedly, your partner and kids will have enough to deal with—try to lighten their burden a bit.

Lastly, write letters to the people you care about. A personal note can offer comfort if you depart without the chance to say goodbye.

Chapter 37

Overcoming Doubts: The Challenge of Writing a Book

Admitting myself into a mental health hospital was a tough decision. At the time, I questioned why I should endure the pain when ending it all seemed like the easier choice. Before my mental breakdown, I admit, I viewed those who took their own lives as selfish and self-centred.

Looking back, I'm shocked by those thoughts. If I had taken that path, I would have missed so many wonderful moments since my breakdown. Spending quality time with my wife, kids, their loved ones, and friends has brought me immense joy and love for life. I also couldn't bear the thought of leaving my family without a shoulder to lean on. It would have been a disaster I can't even begin to describe.

Reflecting on those dark moments, I'm grateful for the support and love that surrounded me during my toughest times. It's incredible how much brighter life can become when we choose to seek help and hold on during the storm.

While the road to recovery hasn't been easy, it's been filled with moments of laughter, love and growth that I wouldn't trade for anything. These experiences have taught me the value of resilience, compassion and cherishing every moment with those who matter most to me.

Today, I'm filled with gratitude for the life I almost missed out on. Every smile, every hug and every moment of connection reminds me of the beauty and preciousness of life. I'm thankful for the strength to seek help when I needed it and for the unwavering support of my loved ones alone the way. While the journey isn't over, I'm hopeful for the future and committed to cherishing each moment as a gift.

As I embark on the journey of writing this book, doubts plagued my mind. Would I ever finish it?

Embarking on the journey of writing a book can be daunting, with doubts and uncertainties clouding the path ahead. I, too, encountered such challenges, questioning whether I could ever finish what I started.

One significant obstacle I faced and continue to face is persistent chest pains. These pains heighten my worries and anxiety, as I am still unsure of their origin. I constantly wonder if they are a sign of a serious health concern, a side effect of medication, or simply my mind playing tricks on me. The chest pains feel very real, reflecting the inner turmoil I still face today. My cardiologist reassures me that these pains are expected and not a cause for concern. When I asked, "Could it be another heart attack?" he replied, "If you think you are having a heart attack, call an ambulance immediately."

The pain feels very real, serving as a physical manifestation of the inner struggles I still confront today.

Sam P

Six months ago, I took a significant step in the creation of this book by sharing a couple of chapters with a close friend of mine. I was eager to hear his thoughts, hoping for some constructive feedback that would guide me as I continued to write. His response, however, was almost immediate and startlingly candid: "I hate it. It's not the Joe I know and love."

His words hit me hard. He explained that the chapters I had shared were too depressing, and that they didn't reflect the person he knew me to be. He urged me to concentrate more on the positive aspects of my experiences rather than the negative ones. This feedback forced me to pause and reassess my approach.

My friend's reaction made me realise just how challenging it can be to strike a balance when writing about deeply personal and often painful experiences. On one hand, it was essential for me to convey the raw truth of my struggles with mental health. Authenticity was crucial; I wanted to ensure that my story could resonate with others facing similar challenges. On the other hand, I also recognised the importance of offering hope and positivity, to ensure that readers didn't feel overwhelmed by the weight of my experiences.

Balancing these two elements proved to be one of the most difficult aspects of writing this book. I wanted to be honest about the lows, the moments of despair and hopelessness, because these are integral parts of the journey through mental health struggles. But I also needed to highlight the moments of joy, the victories, and the lessons learned along the way. I aimed to create a narrative that was both truthful and uplifting, a reflection of the full spectrum of my experiences.

Dear reader, I sincerely hope that I have succeeded in putting a smile on your face, "at times" I have strived to find a middle ground where the darkness of my past is illuminated by the light of hope and resilience. It has been a delicate balancing act, one that needed constant reflection and adjustment.

Writing this book has been as much about understanding and accepting my own experiences as it has been about sharing them with you. It is my hope that through this balance, I have managed to create a story that is not only engaging but also encouraging. I want you to see that while the road can be rough and filled with obstacles, there is always a possibility for brighter days ahead.

Chapter 38

One year on

It has been one year since my discharge from Gilead 4, Ward 7—a milestone that feels both monumental and surreal. The memories of that time are still vivid, etched deeply into my mind. They resurface unexpectedly, reminding me that my journey is far from over.

The turbulence I faced within those walls was like being caught in a relentless storm, with each wave threatening to pull me under. The struggle wasn't just about surviving day to day, but about finding the strength to keep going, even when the waves felt insurmountable.

Now, a year later, I find myself still riding those waves, still grappling with the aftershocks of what I went through. There are days when the waves are calm, where I can breathe and reflect on how far I've come. But there are also days when the waves rise again, threatening to drown me in the memories and emotions that still linger. It's a continuous process of learning and adapting, of finding new ways to cope with this ongoing journey. I've learned that healing isn't linear; it's more like riding a wave—sometimes you're up, sometimes you're down, and sometimes you're just trying to stay afloat. But through it all, I've come to realise that the act of riding the wave is itself a massive step in the right direction. I'm still here, still moving forward, still learning how to navigate those bloody waves.

I’ve often been confronted by the question from friends and loved ones:

“What is your End Game?”
(The last part of a process or action).

Mental Illness is like navigating a treacherous minefield, where every step feels precarious.

In the midst of my struggles, I searched desperately for validation, for something or someone who could echo my feelings and experiences.

Perhaps I wasn’t searching diligently enough, or perhaps the words I sought simply eluded me.

If my book resonates with even just one person, if they find solace in knowing that they’re not alone in their struggles, then that, to me, is my ultimate

“End Game”.

Thank you for allowing me to share my journey with you.

Epilogue

As I conclude this journey, I am reminded of the uncertainties that accompanied me at its start. When I first decided to write this book, doubts plagued my mind. Would I ever finish it? Could I capture the essence of my experiences and translate them into something meaningful for others?

Embarking on the journey of writing a book can indeed be daunting. The path is often clouded with uncertainties, and the destination can seem impossibly distant. Yet, here I am, having completed a project that has been a decade in the making. It took nearly one year of dedicated effort to transform my scattered thoughts and notes into the coherent narrative that lies before you.

Reflecting on this achievement, I am filled with a profound sense of accomplishment. If my book resonates with even just one person, if it provides solace and understanding to someone who feels alone in their struggles, then I consider my efforts to be truly worthwhile. My ultimate goal has always been to shed light on the often-misunderstood terrain of mental health, offering insight and empathy to those navigating similar paths.

Throughout the writing process, I faced many challenges. The journey through mental health is fraught with highs and lows, and I have come to realise that these difficult feelings, while often intense, are usually temporary. It is important to acknowledge that such feelings may never completely disappear. However, their strength and intensity can be alleviated. My hope is that reading this book has given you a head start and a bit more understanding of mental illness.

Even on the days when the demons swirling in my head seem overwhelming, I have learned to ride out the waves, trusting that they will eventually pass. This resilience is something I wish to impart to you, dear reader. No matter how dark the storm may seem, there is always a glimmer of light on the horizon. It might be hard to see at times, but it is there, waiting for you to find it.

As you turn the last page of this book, I wish you good luck and Godspeed*.

Thank you for joining me on this voyage. May you find the strength and courage to face your own demons, we all have them!

*Please note that this term carries no religious connotations in this context. It is simply a salutation wishing you luck and success in your journey ahead.

Confidential Report

Extracts from my latter yearly reports.

He is an outgoing, energetic man, with a decisive manner, determination and faultless attention to detail. He has maintained a firm grip on his staff, and showed outstanding, leadership and compassion. (Battery* Commander - 2002).

He is industrious, outgoing and accepts only the highest of standards. (Quartermaster - 2003).

He has been employed as the Battery G5 SNCO of a Germany based AS90 Battery deployed in the infantry role in Basra city, Iraq as part of the Royal Regiment of Wales Battlegroup on OP TELIC 3. In barracks, he has filled the key post of Battery Training Warrant Officer.

He is smart, gregarious, and earnest individual with an infectious sense of enthusiasm. Professionally driven with a meticulous eye for detail.

He has had an excellent reporting period during which he has been largely responsible for the development from concept to completion of over $1.2 million worth of projects throughout the Battery Area Of Responsibility, which included the infamously downtrodden Shia Flats area.

These projects have been extremely diverse in manner, ranging from the refurbishment of schools to the development of economic infrastructure.

In addition, he has ably understudied the Operations Warrant Officer, during the last month of the tour, where he ably coordinated a series of complex operations against confirmed terrorist targets.

He has produced an excellent performance during a demanding year and sits comfortably at the top of the Senior Non-Commissioned Officers within a strong Battery. (Battery Commander - 2004 - Now a 3 Star Lieutenant General). Correct as of March 2024.

He has been a Troop Sergeant Major and Battery Training Officer in a Gun Battery.

He is forthright, open and honest. He has a natural ability to instil trust, drives himself and others hard while maintaining the knack of being able to judge and respond well to the needs of those around him. His enthusiasm and drive are outstanding.

He has ample initiative and requires little direction. As Battery Training Officer he drove down the training requirements to return the Battery back to Gunnery. As Battery Reconnaissance Officer, he proved his field ability during a live firing exercise. Without his personal input, the leadership course would not have happened. (Battery Commander - 2005).

He has won fulsome praise from the General Officer Commanding and Commander 1 (UK) Armoured Division. In addition, he has proven his technical Field Gunnery competence in Barracks and on a live firing exercise as a Battery Reconnaissance Officer and Gun Line Section Commander. He has the potential to make an excellent Battery Sergeant Major and will serve the gunners well. (Commanding Officer - 2005 - Retired as a 3-star Lieutenant General).

*Battery
A Battery is a team of over 100 soldiers that operates several powerful cannons. These cannons can fire shells (large bullets that weigh 100 pounds - 45 kg - 7 stone) over long distances (24.7 kilometres or 15 miles).

A Battery includes not only the gunners who fire the cannons but also the leaders who choose the targets and other team members who manage communication, supplies and equipment maintenance.

Together, they ensure the cannons are used effectively to support other troops in battle.

Three or four Batteries make up a Regiment, which is commanded by a Lieutenant Colonel.

AS90 - A big cannon on tracks.

Some of the Key jobs within a Battery:

A Battery is Commanded by a Battery Commander (usually a Major) and has a Battery Sergeant Major who assists in administration and discipline.

A Battery Training Officer is responsible for planning and overseeing the training of the Battery's soldiers.

A Battery Reconnaissance Officer in an AS90 Regiment is responsible for scouting and selecting suitable firing positions for the Battery's cannons.

British Army Ranks:

Private/Gunner (Artillery)

- All new soldiers start as Privates/Gunners on completion of Basic Training.
- Depending on the corps or regiment in which they are serving, their title may be Trooper, Gunner, Signaller, Sapper, Guardsman, Rifleman or Kingsman.

Lance Corporal/Lance Bombardier (Artillery)

- Promotion follows Initial Trade Training or about four years serving as a Private.
- Supervises a small team of up to four soldiers called a section.

Corporal/Bombardier (Artillery)

- Promotion after about six to eight years of service and on ability to lead.
- Given command of more soldiers and equipment – such as tanks and guns.

Sergeant

- Senior role of responsibility, with promotion typically taking place after 12 years of service and on ability.
- Typically, second in command of a troop or platoon of up to 35 soldiers, with the important

responsibility for advising and aiding junior officers.

Colour Sergeant/Staff Sergeant (Artillery)

- After a few years as a Sergeant promotion to either Staff or Colour Sergeant.
- This is a senior role combining personnel and resource management of about 120 soldiers or command of a platoon or troop.

Warrant Officer Class 2 (Sergeant Major/Warrant Officer) – "Sir"

- This is a senior management role focusing on the training, welfare and discipline of a company, squadron, or battery of up to 120 soldiers.
- WO2s act as the senior advisors to the Major in command of the sub-unit.

Warrant Officer Class 1 – "Bigger Sir"

- The most senior soldier rank in the British Army.

Officer Ranks

Officer Cadet

- The rank held during initial officer training.

Second Lieutenant

- The lowest commissioned officer rank in the British Army.

- Responsible for leading up to 30 soldiers in a platoon or troop, rank normally held for one to two years.

Lieutenant

- Normally command a platoon or troop of around 30 soldiers, with increased responsibilities from being a Second Lieutenant.
- Typically held for two to three years.

Captain

- Normally made second-in-command of a sub-unit of up to 120 soldiers.
- Typically held for 5 to 10 years.

Major

- Commands a sub-unit of up to 120 officers and soldiers.
- Responsible for their training, welfare and administration both in camp and operations, as well as the management of their equipment.

Lieutenant Colonel

- Commands units of up to 650 soldiers, containing four or five sub-units – known as the Commanding Officer, for typically two years.
- They are responsible for the overall operational effectiveness of their unit in terms of military capability, welfare and general discipline.

Colonel

- Normally serve as staff officers (responsible for the Army's administrative needs) operating between field commands at battalion/brigade level.

Brigadier (one-star)

- Commands a brigade in the field or holds a senior staff appointment.

Major General (two-star)

- Commands a division or brigade

Lieutenant General (three-star)

- Commands formations of corps size and other commands in the UK and overseas.
- Holds very senior staff appointments in the MOD and other headquarters.

General (four-star)

- Currently, the highest rank in the British Army for serving personnel.
- Holds the most senior appointments – such as Chief of Defence Staff, Vice Chief of Defence Staff, Chief of the General Staff, Deputy Supreme Allied Commander Europe, and Commander in Chief Land Forces.

Medical Terminology

What is Medical Terminology?

Medical terminology is the language healthcare professionals use to describe various aspects of health, like diseases, treatments, procedures and body parts. It's like a secret code doctors, nurses and others use to talk efficiently and accurately about health-related topics.

The following bullet points provide a quick reference to the medical terms discussed in my book.

Psychiatrist vs. Psychologist: What's the Difference?

If you're seeking help for mental health issues, you might come across two different types of professionals: psychiatrists and psychologists. While they both work in the field of mental health, there are some key differences between them.

Psychiatrists:

- Psychiatrists are medical doctors who specialise in mental health.
- They can diagnose and treat mental illnesses using a combination of therapy, medication and other medical interventions.
- Psychiatrists can prescribe medication to help manage symptoms of mental health conditions.

- They often work with individuals who have more severe or complex mental health issues, such as schizophrenia, bipolar disorder, or severe depression.

- Psychiatrists may also provide therapy, but their primary focus is on the medical aspects of mental health.

Psychologists:

- Psychologists are mental health professionals who have advanced degrees in psychology.

- They specialise in understanding human behaviour and mental processes.

- Psychologists provide therapy* and counselling to help individuals manage and overcome mental health issues.

- They use various therapeutic approaches, such as cognitive-behavioural therapy (CBT), psychotherapy and other evidence-based techniques.

- Psychologists cannot prescribe medication, but they work closely with psychiatrists and other healthcare providers to coordinate care for their clients.

- Psychologists may work with individuals experiencing a wide range of mental health concerns, from everyday stress and anxiety to more severe conditions.

* To provide therapy, a psychologist needs specialised training in therapy. This involves completing a degree in psychology, focusing on clinical or counselling psychology. In addition to their degree, they must gain supervised clinical experience and obtain certification. Without this specific training and certification, a psychologist cannot legally or ethically offer therapy services.

- **Heart Attack:** This occurs when blood flow to a part of the heart is blocked, usually by a blood clot. It can cause chest pain, shortness of breath and other symptoms.

- **Stroke:** A stroke is a medical emergency that happens when blood flow to a part of the brain is blocked or when a blood vessel in the brain bursts. Without enough blood, the brain cells in that area start to die because they aren't getting the oxygen and nutrients they need. This can cause sudden problems like difficulty speaking, weakness on one side of the body, or trouble seeing. Getting quick treatment is really important to help prevent long-term damage.

- **Defibrillation:** Defibrillation is a medical procedure used to restore normal heart rhythm. It involves delivering an electrical shock to the heart using a device called a defibrillator. This shock helps to depolarise the heart muscle and allows the heart to resume its normal beating pattern. Defibrillation is often performed in emergency situations, such as cardiac arrest, to potentially save a person's life.

- **Atrial Fibrillation (AF) :** AF is a heart condition where the upper chambers of the heartbeat irregularly, leading to symptoms like palpitations and fatigue.

- **Chest Pains:** Chest pains refer to discomfort or pain felt in the chest area, which may vary in intensity and duration. Chest pain can be caused by a variety of factors, including heart-related issues such as angina, heart attack, or pericarditis, as well as other conditions like acid reflux, muscle strain, or respiratory infections. It's important to seek medical attention promptly if experiencing chest pains, especially if accompanied by symptoms such as shortness of breath, dizziness, nausea or sweating as they could show a serious underlying condition.

- **Mental Health Hospital:** A facility that provides treatment and care for individuals experiencing mental health crises or conditions that require intensive monitoring and support.

- **High Blood Pressure (Hypertension):** High blood pressure occurs when the force of blood against the walls of your arteries is consistently too high. It is often referred to as the “silent killer” because it typically has no symptoms but can lead to serious health problems such as heart disease, stroke and kidney failure if left untreated. Monitoring blood pressure regularly and making lifestyle changes or taking medications as prescribed by a healthcare provider can help manage hypertension and reduce the risk of complications.

- **PTSD (Post-Traumatic Stress Disorder):** PTSD is a mental health condition that can develop after experiencing or seeing a traumatic event. Symptoms may include flashbacks, nightmares, severe anxiety and uncontrollable thoughts about the event. Treatment often involves therapy, medication, and support from loved ones.

- **Severe Depression:** Depression is a mood disorder characterised by persistent feelings of sadness, hopelessness and loss of interest in activities. Severe depression can significantly affect daily functioning and may require treatment with therapy, medication, lifestyle changes and support from mental health professionals.

- **Anxiety:** Anxiety disorders involve excessive worry, fear, or apprehension that can interfere with daily life. Symptoms may include restlessness, irritability, muscle tension and difficulty concentrating. Treatment options may include therapy, medication, relaxation techniques and lifestyle changes.

- **A trigger:** A trigger, in the context of mental health, is something that provokes a strong emotional response, often bringing up painful memories or intense feelings. Triggers can vary widely from person to person and can come from many diverse sources. For example, a particular place, such as a location where someone experienced a traumatic event, can serve as a trigger. Similarly, certain sounds, like a loud noise that recalls a past frightening experience, can also act as triggers. Even specific smells, which are strongly linked to memory, can unexpectedly remind someone of a distressing time in their life.

  Additionally, everyday situations or conversations can serve as triggers. For instance, discussing a topic that touches on a person's past trauma or being in a situation that feels like a previously stressful event can bring back those intense emotions. Triggers are highly personal and can vary greatly; what might be a trigger for one person may not affect someone else in the same way. Understanding and identifying triggers is an important part of managing mental health, as it allows individuals to develop coping strategies to deal with the emotional responses that triggers can cause.

- **Hypervigilance:** Hypervigilance is a state of heightened alertness and increased sensitivity to potential threats or danger in one's environment. It is often associated with anxiety disorders, post-traumatic stress disorder (PTSD) and other mental health conditions. Individuals experiencing hypervigilance may be constantly scanning their surroundings, feeling on edge, or easily startled, and have difficulty relaxing or concentrating due to their heightened state of arousal. Hypervigilance can negatively affect daily functioning and quality of life, and may require treatment such as therapy, medication and stress management techniques to alleviate symptoms and improve coping mechanisms.

- **Panic Attacks:** Panic attacks are sudden episodes of intense fear or discomfort that can occur unexpectedly or in response to a trigger. During a panic attack, individuals may experience symptoms such as rapid heartbeat, sweating, trembling, shortness of breath, chest pain, dizziness and feelings of impending doom or loss of control. Panic attacks can be overwhelming and debilitating, often leading to a sense of fear about future attacks and avoidance of certain situations or places. Treatment for panic attacks may include therapy, medication, relaxation techniques and lifestyle changes to help manage symptoms and prevent future episodes.

- **CBT (Cognitive Behavioural Therapy):** CBT is a type of psychotherapy that focuses on identifying and changing negative thought patterns and behaviours. It is commonly used to treat various mental health conditions, including anxiety disorders, depression, post-traumatic stress disorder (PTSD) and phobias. CBT helps individuals develop coping skills, challenge irrational beliefs, and learn healthier ways of thinking and behaving. This therapy is typically short-term and goal-oriented, with the aim of providing practical strategies for managing symptoms and improving overall well-being.

- **Mindfulness:** Mindfulness is a practice that involves paying attention to the present moment with openness, curiosity, and acceptance. It involves focusing on sensations, thoughts and emotions without judgment. Mindfulness techniques, such as meditation and deep breathing exercises, are often used to reduce stress, promote relaxation, improve concentration and enhance overall mental well-being. This practice has been integrated into various forms of therapy, including cognitive-behavioural therapy (CBT), to help individuals manage anxiety, depression, chronic pain and other health conditions.

- **Meditation:** Meditation is like giving your brain a break from all the craziness of life. You know how sometimes your mind feels like it's going a mile a minute, with thoughts bouncing all over the place? Well, meditation helps you slow down and focus on just one thing, like your breath or a calming word. It's not about shutting off your thoughts completely; it's more about noticing them without getting caught up in them. It's like hitting the pause button on the chaos and finding a little oasis of calm inside yourself.

- **Sleep Deprivation:** Sleep deprivation occurs when an individual does not get enough sleep to meet their body's needs. It can result from various factors, including lifestyle choices, medical conditions and sleep disorders. Symptoms of sleep deprivation may include excessive daytime sleepiness, irritability, difficulty concentrating, impaired memory and mood changes. Chronic sleep deprivation can have profound consequences on physical and mental health, increasing the risk of conditions such as obesity, diabetes, cardiovascular disease and depression. Improving sleep hygiene, addressing underlying medical conditions and seeking professional help can help alleviate sleep deprivation and promote better overall health and well-being.

- **Diverticular Disease:** Diverticular disease refers to a group of conditions related to the presence of diverticula, small pouches that can form in the lining of the digestive tract, particularly the colon. Diverticular disease includes diverticulosis, where diverticula are present but not inflamed or infected, and diverticulitis, where the diverticula become inflamed or infected. Symptoms of diverticular disease can vary but may include abdominal pain, bloating, changes in bowel habits and complications such as diverticulitis or bleeding. Treatment may involve dietary modifications, medication to manage symptoms, and in severe cases, surgery. Maintaining a high-fibre diet, staying hydrated and regular exercise can help prevent or manage diverticular disease. Regular medical check-ups are important for checking the condition and preventing complications.

- **Coronary Angiogram:** A coronary angiogram is a medical procedure used to visualise the blood flow in the coronary arteries, which supply oxygen-rich blood to the heart muscle. During a coronary angiogram, a special dye is injected into the bloodstream, and X-ray images are taken to assess the blood flow through the coronary arteries. This procedure helps doctors diagnose and evaluate conditions such as coronary artery disease, blockages and narrowing of the coronary arteries. It is often performed as part of the diagnostic workup for chest pain, heart attack or other heart-related symptoms.

- **Stent Implantation:** Stent implantation is a medical procedure used to treat blockages or narrowing in blood vessels, particularly arteries. During stent implantation, a small mesh-like tube called a stent is inserted into the affected blood vessel to help keep it open and allow for improved blood flow. The stent is typically inserted into the vessel using a catheter, which is guided to the site of the blockage using imaging techniques such as X-rays or ultrasound. Once in place, the stent expands to support the vessel walls and keep adequate blood flow. Stent implantation is commonly used in the treatment of coronary artery disease, peripheral artery disease and other conditions that cause narrowing of the blood vessels.

- **Low Testosterone (Hormone Replacement Treatment):** Low testosterone, refers to a condition in which the body produces insufficient levels of testosterone, the primary male sex hormone. Symptoms of low testosterone may include reduced libido, erectile dysfunction, fatigue, loss of muscle mass and mood changes. Hormone replacement treatment (HRT) involves supplementing testosterone levels through medications such as gels, patches, injections, or oral tablets. HRT aims to alleviate symptoms associated with low testosterone and restore hormonal balance in the body. It is important to consult with a healthcare provider before starting HRT, as it may carry potential risks and side effects.

- **Heart Rehabilitation:** Heart rehabilitation, also known as cardiac rehabilitation, is a program designed to help individuals recover from heart-related conditions or procedures, such as heart attacks, heart surgery or heart failure. This comprehensive program typically includes exercise training, education on heart-healthy lifestyle choices, nutritional counselling and emotional support. The goal of heart rehabilitation is to improve cardiovascular health, reduce the risk of future heart problems, and enhance overall quality of life for individuals with heart conditions. It is often supervised by a multidisciplinary team of healthcare professionals, including cardiologists, nurses, exercise physiologists and dieticians.

- **Hypnotherapist:** A hypnotherapist is a healthcare professional who uses hypnosis as a therapeutic technique to help individuals address a variety of issues, such as managing pain, reducing stress, overcoming phobias, or changing unhealthy habits. Hypnotherapy involves inducing a relaxed state of consciousness, known as a trance, during which the individual is more open to suggestion and can explore subconscious thoughts and behaviours. Hypnotherapists often work in conjunction with other healthcare providers to complement traditional medical treatments and support overall well-being.

- **Bipolar disorder:** During my stay in a mental hospital, my psychiatrist briefly explored the possibility of bipolar disorder, but after two consultations, it was decided that it wasn't the case for me. However, I have mentioned bipolar disorder in my reference pages because I shared a room with a patient who had the condition.

- Bipolar disorder is a mental health condition that affects how you feel and act. People with bipolar disorder have intense mood swings that go from feeling extremely high and full of energy to feeling extremely low and sad. These mood swings are more extreme than the normal ups and downs that everyone goes through.

Tips for Tackling Medical Topics:

1. Ask Questions: Don't hesitate to ask your healthcare provider to explain any terms or concepts you don't understand. They're there to help you, and clear communication is key to your health.

2. Use Online Resources: There are many reliable websites and resources available that explain medical terminology in simple terms. Look for reputable sources like medical organisations or government health websites. National Health Service (NHS) website is without doubt my "go-to" site when it comes to looking for reliable and up-to-date information on health conditions, treatments and general medical advice.

3. Break it Down: When faced with a complex term, break it down into smaller parts. For example, "atrial fibrillation" can be understood as "irregular heart rhythm in the upper chambers."

4. Take notes: It's helpful to take notes during your healthcare journey. Whether it's using a notebook or a note-taking app on your phone, jotting down new medical terms and their meanings can be beneficial. Reviewing your notes regularly can reinforce your understanding of these terms.

5. Additionally, before appointments, write down any questions you have, and during the appointment, take notes on what your doctor says. This way, you

can keep track of vital information and have a record of your healthcare discussions.

6. Finding support is important, but it’s essential to be cautious about where you seek it. While support groups and online communities can provide valuable connections with others who understand your experiences, it’s worth noting that not all online communities are beneficial.

7. Some forums may perpetuate misinformation or offer harmful advice. For instance, I’ve had regrettable experiences on many “depression” forums. Therefore, when joining online communities, prioritise those that foster a supportive and constructive environment, where correct information is shared, and harmful content is avoided.

Conclusion:

Navigating medical terminology can be daunting, especially when you’re already dealing with health challenges. But with patience, curiosity and the right resources, you can start to unravel the mysteries of medical jargon. Remember, you don’t have to become a doctor overnight – just take it one term at a time, and don’t be afraid to reach out for help when you need it.

The NHS website has been my ultimate go-to resource for all my medical questions.

Symptoms of Severe Depression, Anxiety and Post-Traumatic Stress Disorder

Through my own research, primarily from the NHS website, I've learned about some of the symptoms of Severe Depression, Anxiety and Post-Traumatic Stress Disorder (PTSD).

It's important to note that these symptoms can vary from person to person.

Mental illness is a complex and diverse issue. The following pages draw from my own first-hand experiences and extensive research to provide a starting point for understanding this vast subject. While my book only scratches the surface, it aims to offer a foundation for your further exploration.

Severe Depression:

Severe depression is characterised by a range of symptoms that significantly affect an individual's daily life. These symptoms may include experiencing persistent low mood or sadness, feeling a sense of hopelessness and helplessness, and having low self-esteem. Additionally, individuals may find themselves frequently tearful and overwhelmed with feelings of guilt.

Furthermore, severe depression often manifests in irritability and intolerance towards others, making it challenging to keep healthy relationships. Individuals may also experience a profound lack of motivation and interest in activities they once enjoyed. Making decisions becomes arduous, and life may feel devoid of pleasure or meaning. It's not uncommon for those with severe depression to also experience symptoms of anxiety or worry, compounding their distress.

Perhaps most concerning is the thoughts of self-harm or suicide that can go with severe depression. These intrusive thoughts reflect the depth of despair and suffering individuals may endure, underscoring the urgent need for proper support and intervention to ensure their safety and well-being.

Anxiety:

My research on anxiety, particularly generalised anxiety disorder (GAD), has revealed that its symptoms can affect individuals both mentally and physically. The severity of these symptoms varies from person to person, with some experiencing only a few and others experiencing many more.

Psychological symptoms of GAD include feelings of restlessness, a pervasive sense of dread or fear, and a constant feeling of being "on edge." Individuals may struggle with concentration and become easily irritable. These symptoms can lead to changes in behaviour and thinking patterns, causing individuals to withdraw from social interactions and avoid situations that trigger worry and fear.

In addition to psychological symptoms, GAD can manifest in various physical symptoms. These can include dizziness, fatigue, palpitations or a noticeably fast heartbeat, muscle tension, trembling or shaking, dry mouth, excessive sweating, shortness of breath, stomach discomfort, nausea, headaches, pins and needles sensations and difficulty sleeping. These physical symptoms can further worsen feelings of distress and contribute to a cycle of worry and decreased self-esteem.

Post-Traumatic Stress Disorder. PTSD:

Re-experiencing traumatic events is a hallmark symptom of PTSD, often manifesting in involuntary and vivid recollections. Individuals may undergo flashbacks, wherein they feel as though they're reliving the traumatic event, or they may experience distressing nightmares. Additionally, repetitive and distressing images or sensations, as well as physical symptoms like pain, sweating, nausea, or trembling, can further intensify the re-experiencing of trauma.

Furthermore, individuals with PTSD may struggle with constant negative thoughts surrounding their traumatic experience. They may find themselves repeatedly questioning why the event occurred and whether they could have done anything differently to prevent it. These intrusive thoughts hinder their ability to come to terms with the event and can lead to feelings of guilt, shame, or self-blame. This ongoing rumination can significantly affect their emotional well-being and hinder their ability to move forward.

Recognising these symptoms is crucial in identifying and addressing PTSD effectively. By understanding the complex ways in which trauma can affect individuals, healthcare professionals can provide proper support and interventions to help individuals cope with their experiences and work towards healing and recovery.

The following are PDF files that I found extremely helpful from: NHS - Inform

(Please note you may not be able to access this site if you are outside the UK).

To Access the NHS, Inform - PDF Files:

1. In the search bar at the top of the web browser, type "NHS Inform," and press Enter.

2. Click on the link to the NHS Inform website from the search results.

3. Once on the NHS Inform website, find the search box. Type one of the following headings in the search box:

   Depression self-help guide
   Anxiety self-help guide
   PTSD and CPTSD self-help guide
   Problem solving self-help guide
   Problem solving self-help guide — action plan
   Problem solving self-help guide — problem list
   Problem solving self-help guide — solution list

4. When the search results appear, click on the first item that appears.

5. On the selected page, look for a link or button to save and download the PDF file. Click on it and follow the instructions that appear on your computer screen to complete the download.

The following are PDF files that I found extremely helpful from:
NHS - Inform
Click on the black type and click on, "open Link" when it appears.

Depression self-help guide

https://drive.google.com/file/d/1p-mr2A9AnpMUrJVpKKFnbh7NWdD4wxdS/view?usp=drivesdk

Anxiety self-help guide

https://drive.google.com/file/d/1LD7SZDFapHkq0_gHxelIgpk1v0sJXPjI/view?usp=drivesdk

PTSD and CPTSD self-help guide

https://drive.google.com/file/d/1YNAjbcyylnzX7r5EYfpZT-TEjBWRCPAD/view?usp=drivesdk

Problem solving self-help guide

https://drive.google.com/file/d/1lGEaCpxxyIi0RaMT1qVE8RGsfXM5hZ9Z/view?usp=drivesdk

Problem solving self-help guide — action plan

https://drive.google.com/file/d/11GXeMPu_4MYnV_I2vDTDoixaFvVeyNtW/view?usp=drivesdk

Problem solving self-help guide — problem list

https://drive.google.com/file/d/1v9MT4ohHiwcIX2HOg_XH4ni1rXZlDNS3/view?usp=drivesdk

Problem solving self-help guide — solution list

https://drive.google.com/file/d/194mvnqp4yUfibKwofbhBiQaZy1-GLDcy/view?usp=drivesdk

My friend Rob insisted that I include a picture of my medals and a brief description.

The General Service Medal (GSM) - Northern Ireland

Cyprus - United Nations Peacekeeping Force in Cyprus (UNFICYP) medal

Bosnia - NATO Medal with Former Yugoslavia clasp

The Iraq Medal. Operational service in Iraq between 20 January 2003 and 22 May 2011

HM The Queen's Golden Jubilee Medal

The Army Long Service and Good Conduct Medal

Preface - From my second book

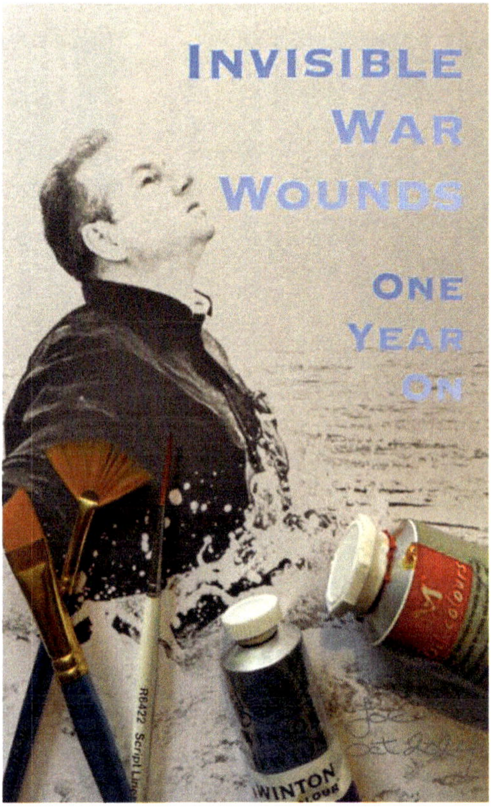

Just a short while ago, I completed my first book, Invisible War Wounds - Life as a British Soldier and my personal Battle with Mental Illness. It marked the end of a year filled with a whirlwind of emotions, a period during which I've been grappling with the realities of Depression, Anxiety and PTSD.

Writing that book became both a distraction and a lifeline—something to cling to amidst the storm. Yet, even as it offered an escape, it was a battle of its own, forcing me to confront the very demons I was trying to understand and overcome.

When I handed a copy of Invisible War Wounds to my sister and my dad, their reactions were immediate and intense. They told me they couldn't put it down and urged me to write another book.

At first, I brushed off the idea. The thought of diving back into that emotional territory felt overwhelming. But as time passed, something shifted within me. I started tossing around ideas—fictional war stories, maybe a murder mystery. Writing a second part to my first book wasn't even on the table. But then, the questions started coming. Friends, acquaintances and even strangers began asking me how I cope—how I manage to "suppress the feelings of shittiness" that linger long after the hospital stay, long after the acute pain has dulled but still remains. They wanted to know how I navigate each day, carrying the weight of my experiences while trying to move forward.

That's when it hit me—a eureka moment if you will. I realised that my journey wasn't over. The story I began in Invisible War Wounds wasn't finished. There was still so much more to explore, to understand, and most importantly, to share. And so, I decided to take on what I knew would be a massive undertaking: writing a diary in book form, documenting my life. Every day, I would chronicle my comings and goings, my thoughts and feelings and the strategies I use to get through each day.

This book is that log. It's an intimate, unfiltered look at what it's like to live with the aftershocks of trauma and mental illness, day by day, moment by moment. It's a continuation of the journey I began in my first book, but it's also something different—a raw, ongoing account of the struggles, small victories and everything in between.

As someone who has worn many hats—soldier, husband, father and self-proclaimed "tough guy"—I never imagined I would face the challenges that came with mental illness. Yet, like so many others, I found myself blindsided.

Writing Invisible War Wounds was about exposing my life to the world, not just as an act of catharsis, but to educate and hopefully, to help others who might be walking a similar path. With this new book, I hope to take that mission even further. By sharing my daily battles, I want to encourage others to take their mental health seriously, to understand that it's not a battle they have to fight alone.

In Invisible War Wounds, I left the reader with these words:

"I'm still here, still moving forward, still learning how to navigate those bloody waves—this chapter is yet to be written."

At the time, I had no intention of writing a second book. I thought that chapter might never be written. But as the saying goes, "never say never." And so, dear reader, here we are, ready to embark on this next chapter together.

Dear Reader, at this time, I do not have a confirmed release date for my upcoming book, Invisible War Wounds - Onc Ycar On, as this project is a journey I have only recently embarked upon.

The following diary entries are excerpts from my forthcoming book. Dear reader, I haven't included them to promote "Book Number Two"—quite the contrary. My intention is simply to offer you a small preview of what lies ahead.

....

"On August 8, 2023, I informed my mental health nurse of my intention to leave the mental hospital within the next 24 hours."

In my new book, One Year On" - My Diary's first entry is Sunday 1st September - 2024.

Day 6

Friday - 6 September

I woke up at 7:15, started the day with a cup of tea, and caught the news. The headline that grabbed my attention was about Germany not the UK, considering sending illegal immigrants to Rwanda. It feels surreal to hear this while reflecting on a war raging just over 1000 km away in Ukraine. Have we learned nothing from history? The idea that people are brutally killing each other is both heart-breaking and infuriating. For goodness' sake, what are we doing?

Mid-morning, I made my way to my doctor's surgery to inquire about the results of my cortisol test. Fortunately, they had arrived, and within ten minutes of walking in, I found myself chatting with my doctor. I couldn't help but reflect on the many troubling stories I've heard about the difficulty of securing a doctor's appointment in the UK. I suspect that my relative ease in accessing medical care is largely due to the fact that I have private health insurance.

Dear Reader, please don't interpret this as, "Me being, Pig Headed" or "Hey look at me - I've got private Health Insurance" I simply find myself in the massively fortunate position of being able to afford private health insurance, thanks to my wife's employment with the government, which provides us with a 50% discount on our health insurance. (I must admit, that sounds more like a sales pitch than a simple fact.) Without this substantial reduction, private health insurance would be beyond our means.

My doctor explained that my cortisol levels were slightly elevated—0.6 too high, to be exact. Normal cortisol levels range from 10 to 20 micrograms per decilitre (mcg/dL), and my reading came in at 20.6. To be honest, I have no idea what a decilitre or mcg/dL actually means! I think a decilitre is one-tenth of a litre, but how that relates to mcg or any of this medical jargon is beyond me—Blah Blah Blah!

Nothing alarming, but he wants to be cautious and has scheduled another test in two weeks to keep an eye on it. We then discussed my worsening feelings of "shittiness," particularly in the mornings. In response, he increased my

Sertraline dosage from 100 mg to 150 mg daily. Now, it's just a waiting game to see if this change makes any difference.

Picked up my veteran friend at midday, and as always, we had a good old chat, setting the world to rights. We arrived at the NAAFI just after 1, and to my surprise, the car park was fuller than I've ever seen it. As we walked in, we were greeted by a fantastic sight—the place was packed with fellow veterans, more than I've ever seen in one gathering. The age range was impressive, too—from what I could tell, mid-twenties (not counting the great-grandkids) all the way to mid-eighties.

Two NAAFI chefs stood behind a makeshift hot plate, ready to serve up an incredible curry spread. I was greeted with a cheerful, "Hi Joe, ready when you are." Without wasting time, I made the announcement that the curry was officially open. Despite the average age being around seventy, it's amazing how fast veterans can move when food is involved! By the time, my friend and I got our plates, most had already dug in. I went for Chicken Korma with rice and a couple of onion bhajis, while my friend—never one to hold back—immediately said, "everything!" Being in a wheelchair, he gets away with murder! I was impressed by how much food could fit on an average-sized NAAFI plate—Chicken Korma, Beef Madras, the vegetarian choice, three bhajis, and a couple of papadums. The food was absolutely outstanding.

After we'd filled our bellies, I tried to catch up with as many vets as I could. Everyone seemed to be in high spirits, sharing stories and reconnecting. There was one recurring comment, though—quite a few vets mentioned how much they'd love a pint of beer with their curry. Sadly, the Family's NAAFI doesn't have a liquor license, so no alcohol is allowed to be drank on the premises.

Afterward, I dropped my friend back home, where we had another moan—nothing of real importance, just venting, which is always nice.

I got home around 18:30 and I polished off the leftover chilli from last night. My wife and I then settled in for our usual evening ritual of TV. We watched the penultimate episode of The Walking Dead, followed by a so-so horror film on Prime. Dear reader, you'll likely hear a lot about our evenings in front of the TV—it's something we do almost every night.

And, of course, it's Friday, so that means Coronation Street—you won't find me missing an episode of Corrie. After typing up a few notes for my diary, I called it a night around midnight.

Day 7

Saturday - 7 September

Dear reader, today unravelled in the most disastrous fashion imaginable. It was my second day on the increased Sertraline dose—an extra 50mg that felt like poison to my mind. I didn't just stumble; I plunged into a dark, suffocating abyss I had thought I'd escaped long ago.

Those terrifying thoughts—the ones that haunted me when I was in the mental health hospital—returned.

For the first time in over a year, they crept back like phantoms, uninvited and relentless. Could it be the extra 50mg? I couldn't point the finger at anything else.

As if the day couldn't spiral further into chaos, we visited my wife's father. Two hours in the car only to arrive at the old people's home that we call, "his home."

His dementia—relentless, cruel—stripped him of recognition. He wanted to die. He didn't even recognise us, and we had to remind him, again and again. Each repetition was like stabbing my wife's heart. I could see it in her eyes. In the restroom, I tried to pull myself together with frantic breathing exercises, but my body betrayed me: sweat pouring, heart pounding, panic surging in waves.

We only lasted another fifteen minutes. People speak of dementia like it's a tragic story—but until you witness it, until you see the light in someone's eyes dim until they beg for an end… it's beyond tragedy.

There was a deadening fog between me and the world, a suffocating numbness that gripped my senses, and my emotions were buried beneath layers of indifference.

I was sinking, deep into that awful, familiar pit. My mind was a storm of hypervigilance—every nerve screaming, every thought twisted into something dark. For a brief moment I even considered going to A&E, a desperate thought that only underscores how unbearable it was.

On the drive back, the air-con blasted on full, cooling the sweat but doing nothing for my tortured thoughts. I couldn't stop obsessing over the Sertraline, the horrible suspicion that this medication was driving me backward, unravelling any progress I had made. In that moment, I decided—no more. I wouldn't take another increased dose.

We got home after two long hours. I lay down, breathing exercises offering only the slightest reprieve. It was just one of those days you can't salvage, a day swallowed whole by misery. I was desperate for sleep, to bury the day in darkness and wake up in a different tomorrow.

But one question lingered: Should I keep writing this diary or let it go?

The question inevitably arises: how did I manage to navigate the overwhelming darkness of this day?

My mental state was one of extreme hypervigilance, where every nerve seemed to be on high alert, and every thought took on a distorted, ominous quality. It felt as though I was once again descending into that deep, familiar abyss. My body responded as if it were in a state of constant "fight or flight." To regain some control, I employed various coping mechanisms, primarily through deep breathing exercises.

These exercises, which I practiced both in the restroom and the car, involved slow, deliberate breaths to calm my racing mind and body. Throughout the day, I repeatedly reminded myself that "this will pass," and that tomorrow would inevitably arrive. I focused on the idea of riding out the emotional storm, knowing that I had been in this place before and had eventually appeared from it.

I vividly remember the first time I was confronted with these intrusive thoughts. The experience was nothing short of terrifying—an unprecedented assault on my mental and emotional well-being. It was unlike anything I had ever encountered before, and the intensity of the emotions left me feeling utterly demoralised. The emotional pain was profound, almost unbearable, and it engulfed me in a way that is difficult to fully articulate.

There is often a common narrative surrounding mental health that suggests earlier experience with such thoughts can serve as a resource or asset. One might say, "The good news is, I've faced these thoughts before and now know how to cope." In theory, familiarity with such experiences should provide a sense of preparedness or resilience. However, in reality, I find little solace in having been through this before.

The fact that I have endured these thoughts previously does not lessen their impact when they re-emerge. Rather, I find myself wishing I had never had to confront them at all.

As I revisit my entry from Day 7 several times, I am struck by the rawness of the emotions I described. A part of me is tempted to dismiss those feelings as overly dramatic—a reaction that would have been characteristic of my mindset over a year ago. However, I must emphasise that there is no exaggeration in what I describe. These thoughts and feelings are not the product of melodrama; they are real, visceral, and deeply impactful. Only those who have endured the turmoil of mental illness can truly understand the depth of these experiences.

Mental illness is a relentless and cruel adversary. It strips away one's sense of control and distorts reality in ways that can be both isolating and devastating. There is no underestimating the seriousness of these struggles. To dismiss them as mere theatrics would be to undermine the very real suffering that goes with mental health challenges.

Dear reader, I must confess that my first inclination was to leave this day blank.

The thought of documenting the events felt overwhelming, and I was prepared to omit them entirely. Yet, upon reflection, I realised that such an omission would be a disservice—not only to myself but to you.

A few days later, a sense of guilt crept in, a guilt rooted in the realisation that by withholding my experience, I would be failing in my commitment to honesty. To neglect sharing the depth of my emotional turmoil would be to obscure the reality of my journey. It is important that I convey this, particularly if you, by chance, are walking a similar path.

I must be candid—this day was one marked by profound feelings of despondency and emotional disarray. To pretend otherwise would distort the truth of my experience.

I share this not to burden you, but rather to remind you that days like this can and do happen, even in the context of recovery.

Should you find yourself facing a similar challenge, know that you are not alone. Stay strong, my friend.

Invisible War Wounds
One Year On

COMING SOON

About the author

Joe was born in the vibrant city of Liverpool in 1968 and joined the British Army at just 16 years old. After 24 years of service, he settled in Germany, in his dream house he calls, 'The White House' - just a short drive from his last posting in Gütersloh. Still happily married after 32 years, Joe and his wife have two boys, Tom and Sam.

As a former British soldier, Joe has faced both visible and invisible wounds. Like many who have served, he once believed that mental illness was something that happened to other people - certainly not someone "hard as nails" like himself. But after leaving the military, he was blindsided by depression, anxiety and PTSD, fighting a battle he never saw coming.

His debut book, Invisible War Wounds: Life as a British Soldier and My Personal Battle with Mental Illness, offers an unfiltered and deeply personal account of his struggles, from holding a senior management position in the British Army to experiencing some of the darkest moments of his mental health journey.

Joe is now dedicated to raising awareness and breaking the stigma surrounding mental illness. To support this cause, he donates proceeds from his book to Combat Stress UK and the mental health hospital where he spent six weeks in recovery. Through his writing, Joe hopes to provide insight, support and encouragement to fellow veterans as well as to the families, friends and loved ones of those fighting their own unseen battles.

He has made it his mission to ensure that when he puts pen to paper, he is speaking directly to you, dear reader - reminding you that:

"you are not alone"

Printed in Dunstable, United Kingdom

77956466R00181